THE OFFICIAL LSAT®
HAND**BOOK**™

The Law School Admission Council (LSAC) is a critical partner for law schools and prospective law students throughout the world. From administering the Law School Admission Test to compiling transcripts, evaluations, letters of recommendation, and applications, LSAC eases the admission process—giving you more time to focus on your future. Learn more about the LSAT and all of LSAC's services for prospective law students at LSAC.org.

A Publication of the Law School Admission Council, Newtown, PA

The Law School Admission Council (LSAC) is a nonprofit corporation that provides unique, state-of-the-art admission products and services to ease the admission process for law schools and their applicants worldwide. Currently, 218 law schools in the United States, Canada, and Australia are members of the Council and benefit from LSAC's services.

© 2010 by Law School Admission Council, Inc.

LSAT, *The Official LSAT PrepTest*, *The Official LSAT SuperPrep*, *ItemWise*, and LSAC are registered marks of the Law School Admission Council, Inc. Law School Forums, LLM Law School Forum, Credential Assembly Service, CAS, LLM Credential Assembly Service, and LLM CAS are service marks of the Law School Admission Council, Inc. *10 Actual, Official LSAT PrepTests*; *10 More Actual, Official LSAT PrepTests*; *The Next 10 Actual, Official LSAT PrepTests*; *10 New Actual, Official LSAT PrepTests with Comparative Reading*; *ABA-LSAC Official Guide to ABA-Approved Law Schools*; Whole Test Prep Packages; *The Official LSAT Handbook*; ACES^2; FlexApp; Candidate Referral Service; DiscoverLaw.org; Law School Admission Test; and Law School Admission Council are trademarks of the Law School Admission Council, Inc.

All rights reserved. No part of this work, including information, data, or other portions of the work published in electronic form, may be reproduced or transmitted in any form or by any means, electronic or mechanical, including photocopying, recording, or by any information storage and retrieval system, without permission of the publisher. For information, write: Communications, Law School Admission Council, 662 Penn Street, PO Box 40, Newtown, PA 18940-0040.

LSAC fees, policies, and procedures relating to, but not limited to, test registration, test administration, test score reporting, misconduct and irregularities, Credential Assembly Service (CAS), and other matters may change without notice at any time. Up-to-date LSAC policies and procedures are available at LSAC.org.

ISBN-13: 978-0-9821487-5-4

Print number
10 9 8 7 6 5 4 3 2

TABLE OF CONTENTS

FOREWORD

In the section of this book titled "A Guide to Analytical Reasoning Questions," the test items discussed were adapted from the December 1992 LSAT, Section 1, questions 1–6.

In the two sections of this book titled, "A Guide to Logical Reasoning Questions" and "A Guide to Reading Comprehension Questions," the test items discussed were taken from previous LSAT administrations that were subsequently published as LSAT PrepTests. They are: PrepTests 10–16, PrepTest 18, PrepTest 20, PrepTests 34–38, PrepTest 52, and PrepTests 54–57. These PrepTests are available for purchase on the LSAC.org website and also may be included in other LSAC test preparation books.

Note: This handbook contains LSAT guide material that is also included in *The Official LSAT SuperPrep*. The guide material in *The Official LSAT Handbook* has been expanded and updated since it was first published in *The Official LSAT SuperPrep*.

INTRODUCTION TO THE LSAT

The LSAT is a half-day, standardized test required for admission to all ABA-approved law schools, most Canadian law schools, and many other law schools. It provides a standard measure of acquired reading and verbal reasoning skills that law schools can use as one of several factors in assessing applicants.

The test consists of five, 35-minute sections of multiple-choice questions. Four of the five sections contribute to the test taker's score. These sections include one Analytical Reasoning section, one Reading Comprehension section, and two Logical Reasoning sections. The unscored section, commonly referred to as the variable section, typically is used to pretest new test questions or to preequate new test forms. The placement of this section in the LSAT will vary. A 35-minute writing sample is administered at the end of the test. The writing sample is not scored by LSAC, but copies are sent to all law schools to which you apply. The score scale for the LSAT is 120 to 180.

The LSAT is designed to measure skills considered essential for success in law school: the reading and comprehension of complex texts with accuracy and insight; the organization and management of information and the ability to draw reasonable inferences from it; the ability to think critically; and the analysis and evaluation of the reasoning and arguments of others.

THE THREE LSAT MULTIPLE CHOICE QUESTION TYPES

The multiple-choice questions that make up most of the LSAT reflect a broad range of academic disciplines and are intended to give no advantage to candidates from a particular academic background.

The five sections of the test contain three different question types. The following material presents a general discussion of the nature of each question type and some strategies that can be used in answering them.

Analytical Reasoning Questions

Analytical Reasoning questions are designed to assess the ability to consider a group of facts and rules, and—given those facts and rules—determine what could or must be true. The specific scenarios associated with these questions are usually unrelated to law since they are intended to be accessible to a wide range of test takers. However, the skills tested parallel those involved in

determining what could or must be the case given a set of regulations, the terms of a contract, or the facts of a legal case in relation to the law. In Analytical Reasoning questions, you are asked to reason deductively from a set of statements and rules or principles that describe relationships among persons, things, or events.

Analytical Reasoning questions appear in sets, each set based on a single passage. The passage used for each set of questions describes common ordering relationships or grouping relationships, or a combination of both types. Examples include scheduling employees for work shifts, assigning instructors to class sections, ordering tasks according to priority, and distributing grants for projects.

Analytical Reasoning questions test a range of deductive reasoning skills. These include:

- Comprehending the basic structure of a set of relationships by determining a complete solution to the problem posed (for example, an acceptable seating arrangement of all six diplomats around a table)

- Reasoning with conditional ("if-then") statements and recognizing logically equivalent formulations of such statements

- Inferring what could be true or must be true from given facts and rules

- Inferring what could be true or must be true from given facts and rules together with new information in the form of an additional or substitute fact or rule

- Recognizing when two statements are logically equivalent in context by identifying a condition or rule that could replace one of the original conditions while still resulting in the same possible outcomes

Analytical Reasoning questions reflect the kinds of detailed analyses of relationships and sets of constraints that a law student must perform in legal problem solving. For example, an Analytical Reasoning passage might describe six diplomats being seated around a table, following certain rules of protocol as to who can sit where. You, the test taker, must answer questions about the logical implications of given and new information. For example, you may be asked who can sit between diplomats X and Y, or who cannot sit next to X if W sits next to Y. Similarly, if you were a student in law school, you might be asked to analyze a scenario involving a set of particular circumstances and a set of governing rules in the form of constitutional provisions, statutes, administrative codes, or prior rulings that have been upheld. You might then be asked to determine the legal options in the scenario: what is required given the scenario, what is permissible given the scenario, and what is prohibited given the scenario. Or you might be asked to develop a "theory" for the case: when faced with an incomplete set of facts about the case, you must fill in the picture based on what is implied by the facts that are known. The problem could be elaborated by the addition of new information or hypotheticals.

No formal training in logic is required to answer these questions correctly. Analytical Reasoning questions are intended to be answered using knowledge, skills, and reasoning ability generally expected of college students and graduates.

Further discussion of Analytical Reasoning questions, including a discussion of different varieties of these questions and strategies for answering them, can be found on pages 6–19.

Logical Reasoning Questions

Arguments are a fundamental part of the law, and analyzing arguments is a key element of legal analysis. Training in the law builds on a foundation of basic reasoning skills. Law students must draw on the skills of analyzing, evaluating, constructing, and refuting arguments. They need to be able to identify what information is relevant to an issue or argument and what impact further evidence might have. They need to be able to reconcile opposing positions and use arguments to persuade others.

Logical Reasoning questions evaluate the ability to analyze, critically evaluate, and complete arguments as they occur in ordinary language. The questions are based on short arguments drawn from a wide variety of sources, including newspapers, general interest magazines, scholarly publications, advertisements, and informal discourse. These arguments mirror legal reasoning in the types of arguments presented and in their complexity, though few of the arguments actually have law as a subject matter.

Each Logical Reasoning question requires you to read and comprehend a short passage, then answer one question (or, rarely, two questions) about it. The questions are designed to assess a wide range of skills involved in thinking critically, with an emphasis on skills that are central to legal reasoning.

These skills include:

- Recognizing the parts of an argument and their relationships

- Recognizing similarities and differences between patterns of reasoning

- Drawing well-supported conclusions

- Reasoning by analogy

- Recognizing misunderstandings or points of disagreement

- Determining how additional evidence affects an argument

- Detecting assumptions made by particular arguments

- Identifying and applying principles or rules

- Identifying flaws in arguments

- Identifying explanations

The questions do not presuppose specialized knowledge of logical terminology. For example, you will not be expected to know the meaning of specialized terms such as "ad hominem" or "syllogism." On the other hand, you will be expected to understand and critique the reasoning contained in arguments. This requires that you possess a university-level understanding of widely used concepts such as argument, premise, assumption, and conclusion.

Further discussion of Logical Reasoning questions, including a discussion of different varieties of these questions and strategies for answering them, can be found on pages 20–45.

Reading Comprehension Questions

Both law school and the practice of law revolve around extensive reading of highly varied, dense, argumentative and expository texts (for example, cases, codes, contracts, briefs, decisions, evidence). This reading must be exacting, distinguishing precisely what is said from what is not said. It involves comparison, analysis, synthesis, and application (for example, of principles and rules). It involves drawing appropriate inferences, and applying ideas and arguments to new contexts. Law school reading also requires the ability to grasp unfamiliar subject matter and the ability to penetrate difficult and challenging material.

The purpose of LSAT Reading Comprehension questions is to measure the ability to read, with understanding and insight, examples of lengthy and complex materials similar to those commonly encountered in law school. The Reading Comprehension section of the LSAT contains four sets of reading questions, each set consisting of a selection of reading material followed by five to eight questions. The reading selection in three of the four sets consists of a single reading passage; the other set contains two related shorter passages. Sets with two passages are a variant of Reading Comprehension called Comparative Reading, which was introduced in June 2007.

Comparative Reading questions concern the relationships between the two passages, such as those of generalization/instance, principle/application, or point/counterpoint. Law school work often requires reading two or more texts in conjunction with each other and understanding their relationships. For example, a law student may read a trial court decision together with an appellate court decision that overturns it, or identify the fact pattern from a hypothetical suit together with the potentially controlling case law.

Reading selections for LSAT Reading Comprehension questions are drawn from a wide range of subjects in the humanities, the social sciences, the biological and physical sciences, and areas related to the law. Generally, the selections are densely written, use high-level vocabulary, and contain sophisticated argument or complex rhetorical structure (for example, multiple points of view). Reading Comprehension questions require you to read carefully and accurately, to determine the relationships among the various parts of the reading selection, and to draw reasonable inferences from the material in the selection. The questions may ask about the following characteristics of a passage or pair of passages:

- The main idea or primary purpose

- Information that is explicitly stated

- Information or ideas that can be inferred

- The meaning or purpose of words or phrases as used in context

- The organization or structure

- The application of information in the selection to a new context

- Principles that function in the selection

- Analogies to claims or arguments in the selection

- An author's attitude as revealed in the tone of a passage or the language used

- The impact of new information on claims or arguments in the selection

Further discussion of Reading Comprehension questions, including a discussion of different varieties of these questions and strategies for answering them can be found on pages 46–72.

The Writing Sample

On the day of the test, you will be asked to write one sample essay. LSAC does not score the writing sample, but copies are sent to all law schools to which you apply. According to a 2006 LSAC survey of 157 United States and Canadian law schools, almost all use the writing sample in evaluating at least some applications for admission. Failure to respond to writing sample prompts and frivolous responses have been used by law schools as grounds for rejection of applications for admission.

In developing and implementing the writing sample portion of the LSAT, LSAC has operated on the following premises: First, law schools and the legal profession value highly the ability to communicate effectively in writing. Second, it is important to encourage potential law students to develop effective writing skills. Third, a sample of an applicant's writing, produced under controlled conditions, is a potentially useful indication of that person's writing ability. Fourth, the writing sample can serve as an independent check on other writing submitted by applicants as part of the admission process. Finally, writing samples may be useful for diagnostic purposes related to improving a candidate's writing.

The writing prompt presents a decision problem. You are asked to make a choice between two positions or courses of action. Both of the choices are defensible, and you are given criteria and facts on which to base your decision. There is no "right" or "wrong" position to take on the topic, so the quality of each test taker's response is a function not of which choice is made, but of how well or poorly the choice is supported and how well or poorly the other choice is criticized.

The LSAT writing prompt was designed and validated by legal education professionals. Since it involves writing based on fact sets and criteria, the writing sample gives applicants the opportunity to demonstrate the type of argumentative writing that is required in law school, although the topics are usually nonlegal.

You will have 35 minutes in which to plan and write an essay on the topic you receive. Read the topic and the accompanying directions carefully. You will probably find it best to spend a few minutes considering the topic and organizing your thoughts before you begin writing. In your essay, be sure to develop your ideas fully, leaving time, if possible, to review what you have written. Do not write on a topic other than the one specified. Writing on a topic of your own choice is not acceptable.

No special knowledge is required or expected for this writing exercise. Law schools are interested in the reasoning, clarity, organization, language usage, and writing mechanics displayed in your essay. How well you write is more important than how much you write. Confine your essay to the blocked, lined area on the front and back of the separate Writing Sample Response Sheet. Only that area will be reproduced for law schools. Be sure that your writing is legible.

A GUIDE TO ANALYTICAL REASONING QUESTIONS

HOW TO APPROACH ANALYTICAL REASONING QUESTIONS

In working through an Analytical Reasoning section of the LSAT, you'll want to do two things: get the answer to the questions right, and use your time efficiently. In this section, you'll get advice on how to do both.

Analytical Reasoning questions test your ability to reason within a given set of circumstances. These circumstances are described in the "setup." A setup consists of sets of elements (people, places, objects, tasks, colors, days of the week, and so on) along with a list of conditions designed to impose some sort of structure or organization on these elements (for example, putting them into an ordered sequence from first to last, selecting subgroups from a larger group, or pairing elements from one set with elements from another set). The different structures allowed by the setup are the "outcomes."

Consider the following setup:

Each of five students—Hubert, Lori, Paul, Roberta, and Sharon—will visit exactly one of three cities— Montreal, Toronto, or Vancouver—for the month of March, according to the following conditions:
  Sharon visits a different city than Paul.
  Hubert visits the same city as Roberta.
  Lori visits Montreal or else Toronto.
  If Paul visits Vancouver, Hubert visits Vancouver with him.
  Each student visits one of the cities with at least one of the other four students.

This setup features two sets of elements: a set of five students and a set of three cities. There are five conditions that constrain how the members of these two sets are associated with each other. The kind of structure that is to be imposed on the elements is this: each student must be paired with exactly one of the cities in strict accordance with the conditions.

> **NOTE.** Analytical Reasoning setups all have one crucial property in common: there is always more than one acceptable outcome. For instance, in the example involving students and the cities they visit, the conditions do not work together to restrict each of the students to visiting a particular city and no other. Instead, there is more than one outcome that satisfies all of the requirements of the setup.

Analytical Reasoning questions test your ability to determine what is necessary, what is possible, and what is impossible within the circumstances of the setup. The types of questions that you are likely to be asked are ones like these:

> *Which one of the following must be true?*
> *Which one of the following could be false?*
> *If Sharon visits Vancouver, which one of the following must be true?*
> *If Hubert and Sharon visit a city together, which one of the following could be true?*

In other words, you'll need to determine what can or must happen, either in general or else in specified circumstances (such as Sharon visiting Vancouver or Hubert and Sharon visiting a city together). And now we'll look at how you go about doing this.

Figuring Out the Setup

The first thing you need to get very clear about is what exactly is supposed to happen to the elements in the setup. So first you need to recognize which parts of the setup serve only as background information.

In the example above, the five students and the three cities are the things you have to associate with one another. What happens to them makes the difference between one outcome and another. But the month of March is merely background information, as is the fact that the visitors are all students. The overall setup allows for a number of different arrangements for the visits. But none of the differences is in any way related to the fact that the visits happen in March, just as none of the differences is in any way related to the fact that the visitors are students. The month could just as well have been April, and the visitors could just as well have been professors or tourists. Changing these things would not change the way the setup and the questions function.

Now, what happens to the elements in the setup? Looking at the students first, you find that each of them is to visit just one of the cities. Looking at the cities, you might at first assume that each city will be visited by at least one of the students. However, notice that there is actually nothing that says that each of the cities has to be visited. Consider the implications of the last condition. This condition essentially says that no student can visit a city alone. This means that, for all three cities to be visited by at least two students, there would have to be at least six students. In actual fact, there are only five. So you know that there cannot be student visitors in all three cities. And the first of the conditions tells you that the students cannot all visit the same city, since Sharon and Paul cannot visit the same city as each other.

So you now know, in general outline, what an acceptable outcome will look like: one of the three cities will be visited by three of the students, one of them by two, and one of them by none. This is the type of implication that can be very useful to work out as you read the conditions, even before you start to answer the questions. It underscores the importance of reading through the setup carefully in order to determine its implications and understand how it works.

HOW TO REPRESENT WHAT HAPPENS (SOME TIME-SAVING TIPS)

Because you've worked out some of the implications of the setup, you now have an idea of the basic shape of the acceptable outcomes. At this point, it might be possible for some people to figure out the answers to individual questions in their heads. Generally, however, this requires enormous powers of concentration and creates opportunities for error. For most people, trying to work these problems in their heads would be an extremely bad idea. Virtually everyone is well advised to use pencil and paper in solving Analytical Reasoning questions.

The time allotted for Analytical Reasoning questions gives you an average of less than 1½ minutes per question. Time management, therefore, is important. Since it does take time to sketch out solutions on paper, you should do whatever you can to use your time economically. Here are some time-saving tips that many people find useful:

- Abbreviate the elements by using just their initials. The elements in lists of names or places or objects will usually have different initials. When elements such as days of the week don't have different initials, be ready to devise abbreviations that will allow you to distinguish them. (For example, in a set of questions involving days of the week, you might use "T" for "Tuesday" and "Th" for "Thursday.")

- Just as you would use initials to represent the elements, you should work with shorthand versions of the conditions. Familiarize yourself with the most common types of conditions and devise your own shorthand way of representing them. For example, one frequent kind of condition stipulates that something that happens to one member of a pair of elements also happens to the other member. In the example above, the condition saying that "Hubert visits the same city as Roberta" is of this type. You might decide that your shorthand for this condition will be "H = R." And for the condition that reads, "If Paul visits Vancouver, Hubert visits Vancouver with him," you might use "if Pv then Hv" or "P(V)→H(V)."

Your shorthand versions of the conditions are the versions that you will be working with, so make sure that they correctly represent what the original conditions actually mean. The time spent in setting the conditions down in this way is likely to be more than offset by the time you'll save through the economy of working with the conditions in a form in which they can be quickly and easily taken in at a glance.

NOTE. It doesn't matter whether anyone else would be able to look at your abbreviations and make sense of them. All that matters is that you yourself become fully fluent in using your abbreviations, so that you can save time when you put things down on paper. Practice doing Analytical Reasoning questions using your own abbreviations. Pick abbreviations that make sense to you. Pick ones that are distinct enough that you won't mistake one for another, especially under the time pressure of taking the test.

- A quick check of the abbreviated setup conditions will sometimes show that one or more of the elements in the setup isn't mentioned in any of the conditions. Don't take this as an indication that there must be a mistake somewhere. Rather, take it at face value: those elements are not specifically constrained. You might devise a special notation for this situation. For example, you could circle those initials and include them at the bottom of your list of setup conditions. Or you might just make a shorthand list of all the elements, whether they are mentioned in the conditions or not.

- In your shorthand system, find a striking way to represent what **cannot** happen. For example, if you encounter a condition of the form "Greg cannot give the first presentation," this might be simply abbreviated as "G not 1" or even "*G(1)," where the asterisk is the symbol you use to represent "not."

- You might find it useful to represent certain conditions in more than one form. For example, you may decide that whenever you find a condition like "If Paul is selected, Raoul is also selected," you will automatically put down, as your shorthand version, both "P→R" and "not R→not P," since (as you'll see later) the two are logically equivalent and you might find it helpful to be reminded of this fact when you're answering the questions.

- For some questions, you might find that it is helpful to quickly write out your abbreviations for the active elements in the set—H L P R S, for example—before you begin to work out the solution. Then you can cross out each element as you satisfy yourself that you have accounted for it in the current solution. This method is especially helpful if the list of elements is too long for you to keep track of it in your head or if you have already marked up your original list of elements.

USING DIAGRAMS

Once you've mapped out the general structure of what's going on in the setup, you can use what you know to construct simple diagrams to help in answering the questions. For example, suppose you have a setup that involves assigning individuals to teams. Here you could use team names as headers and list team members as entries under those headers.

Try to think a bit about which diagramming techniques are effective for you. Consider again the case of the setup involving students and cities. Here you might diagram an outcome with labeled rows, like this:

```
M:  H, R, S
T:  L, P
V:
```

Or you might diagram it with labeled columns, like this:

<u>M</u>	<u>T</u>	<u>V</u>
H, R, S	L, P	

But you probably won't want to end up with a diagram that pairs each student with a city, like this:

<u>H</u>	<u>L</u>	<u>P</u>	<u>R</u>	<u>S</u>
M	T	T	M	M

Although this last diagram presents the same information as the other two, it does so less usefully. For example, the last diagram does not capture as clearly as the other two diagrams do that there is one city that isn't visited by any of the students.

Develop strategies ahead of time that will lead you to create diagrams that are clear and easy for you to work with. There is no one right way to do this, just as there is no one right way to abbreviate conditions. The only way to find out what works best for you is to practice diagramming a number of setups before taking the test.

> **NOTE.** For suggestions and tips on diagramming, see Appendix A, Using Diagrams in Answering Analytical Reasoning Questions, on pages 73–82.

ORIENTATION QUESTIONS

Most Analytical Reasoning sets begin with a question in which each answer choice represents a complete outcome, or sometimes just part of an outcome. These questions ask you to select the single answer choice that is an acceptable outcome (that is, one that doesn't violate any part of the setup). You can think of these as "orientation questions" since they do a good job of orienting you to the setup conditions.

For such questions, probably the most efficient approach is to take each condition in turn and check to see whether any of the answer choices violates it. As soon as you find an answer choice that violates a condition, you should eliminate that answer choice from further consideration—perhaps by crossing it out in your test booklet. When you have run through all of the setup conditions in this fashion, one answer choice will be left that you haven't crossed out: that is the correct answer.

Here's an orientation question relating to the setup in the example:

Which one of the following could be true?

(A) *Hubert, Lori, and Paul visit Toronto, and Roberta and Sharon visit Vancouver.*
(B) *Hubert, Lori, Paul, and Roberta visit Montreal, and Sharon visits Vancouver.*
(C) *Hubert, Paul, and Roberta visit Toronto, and Lori and Sharon visit Montreal.*
(D) *Hubert, Roberta, and Sharon visit Montreal, and Lori and Paul visit Vancouver.*
(E) *Lori, Paul, and Sharon visit Montreal, and Hubert and Roberta visit Toronto.*

Let's take the setup conditions in order from first to last. First, check the first condition against each option:

Condition 1: Sharon visits a different city than Paul.

Condition 1 is met in (A) through (D) but violated in (E), since in (E) Sharon is scheduled to visit the same city as Paul. So you cross out (E) and do not check it any further. Now take the second condition:

Condition 2: Hubert visits the same city as Roberta.

Condition 2 is violated in (A), since in (A) Hubert is scheduled to visit a different city than Roberta. Cross out (A) and don't consider it any further. Condition 2 is not violated in (B), (C), or (D). (Remember, you don't need to

check (E) since you've already ruled it out.) Proceed in the same way with the rest of the conditions:

Condition 3: Lori visits Montreal or else Toronto.

Condition 4: If Paul visits Vancouver, Hubert visits Vancouver with him.

Condition 5: Each student visits one of the cities with at least one of the other four students.

Condition 3 is violated in (D), since in (D) Lori is scheduled to visit Vancouver. Cross out (D). Condition 4 is violated in neither (B) nor (C), the only answer choices you are still checking. (The fact that condition 4 is violated in (D) is irrelevant at this point: you've already crossed out (D).) This leaves condition 5 to decide between (B) and (C). Condition 5 is violated in (B), since in (B) Sharon is scheduled to be the lone student visitor to Vancouver. Thus (B) gets crossed out. The only answer choice not crossed out is (C), which is consequently the correct answer. No further checking of (C) is needed. You've already checked (C) against each of the setup conditions. You are done. With this sort of question, there is no need for diagramming; all you needed to refer to was your abbreviated list of the conditions.

Another way of approaching an orientation question is to consider each answer choice in turn to see whether it violates any of the conditions. This will lead you to the correct answer relatively quickly if the correct answer is (A), and less quickly the further down the correct answer is. On balance, this is probably a less efficient way of finding the answer to an orientation question. Efficiency matters, because the more time you can save doing relatively straightforward questions such as these, the more time you have available to solve more challenging questions.

CAUTION. The method of checking each condition against the answer choices is what you want to use with orientation questions. However, as you'll see below, this is generally not the approach you'll want to take with other types of questions. Keep in mind that your objective in answering the questions is to select the correct answer and move on to the next question, not to prove that the incorrect answer choices are wrong. (Also remember that not every set of questions includes an orientation question. When there is an orientation question, it will always be the question right after the setup.)

QUESTIONS THAT INCLUDE THE PHRASE "ANY ONE OF WHICH"

Another kind of question is concerned with complete and accurate lists of elements "any one of which" has some specific characteristic. A question of this kind might ask:

Which one of the following is a complete and accurate list of students any one of which could visit Vancouver?

The answer choices might be:

(A) Hubert, Lori, Roberta
(B) Hubert, Roberta, Sharon
(C) Paul, Roberta, Sharon
(D) Hubert, Paul, Roberta, Sharon
(E) Hubert, Lori, Paul, Roberta, Sharon

What this question asks you to do is take each of the students in the setup and ask, "Could he or she visit Vancouver?" It doesn't matter whether any of the other students on the list could also visit Vancouver at the same time. You just need to ask whether there is an acceptable outcome in which the student you're considering visits Vancouver. If the answer is yes, that student needs to be included on the list, and if the answer is no, that student needs to stay off the list. If you do this systematically and correctly, the list you eventually end up with will be complete: no student who belongs on that list will have been left out. And it will be accurate: the list will not include any student who does not belong there. The correct answer is the list of all the students for whom the answer is "yes."

Sometimes the task of checking individually whether each element in the setup belongs on this list may seem daunting, but the task can often be simplified. For example, looking at the setup conditions, you notice that the third condition bars Lori from visiting Vancouver. So the two answer choices that include Lori—(A) and (E)—can immediately be crossed out.

Similarly, the second condition directly rules out (C). Condition 2 requires that Hubert visit the same city as Roberta, so if you know that it is possible for one of them to visit Vancouver, it must be possible for the other to visit Vancouver too. This is what the condition requires. So (C), which includes Roberta but not Hubert, is either incomplete or inaccurate.

This leaves you with (B) and (D). They both include Hubert, Roberta, and Sharon. **Don't waste time checking these elements.** Since you have already determined that they are bound to be part of the correct answer, none of them will help you determine which of the remaining two answer choices is the correct one.

> **NOTE.** In general, when dealing with questions that include the phrase "any one of which," there is no point in checking an element that appears in all of the answer choices that you are still considering. It can't help you tell the correct answer from the incorrect ones.

Since the only thing that distinguishes (B) from (D) is that (D) includes Paul, the only point you need to check is whether Paul can visit Vancouver. Since he can, (B) is incomplete and thus incorrect. The correct answer is (D). In this case, when it came down to just (B) and (D), it turned out that checking one element was enough to allow you to identify the correct answer. If it had turned out that Paul could not visit Vancouver, then the correct answer would have been (B). As this case illustrates, it is generally worth your while to use time-saving strategies.

> **NOTE.** In questions that include the phrase "any one of which," if some element appears in only one of the answer choices still under consideration, check that element first. That way, if this element does belong on the list, you are done. Since any list, in order to be complete, would have to include this element, the answer choice that contains this element is the correct answer.

QUESTIONS THAT ASK ABOUT WHAT MUST BE TRUE

Many Analytical Reasoning questions ask about what must be true. Something that must be true is something that is true of every single acceptable outcome. In other words, there **cannot** be an acceptable outcome in which this thing is false. But this does not mean—and this is an important point—that to find the correct answer you should somehow mechanically draw up all of the acceptable outcomes and then look through them to identify the one answer choice that these outcomes all have in common. Don't try to do this.

The reason you should avoid determining all of the acceptable outcomes is not that it will give incorrect results. If used with care and without error, it will lead you to the correct answer. The problem is that it is usually far too time-consuming.

So what should you do instead? This depends on the form of the question. Does the question ask what must be true under certain specified circumstances, or does it ask what must be true on the basis of the setup alone, no matter what the circumstances are? Let's take a look at each of these two possibilities separately.

What Must Be True Under Certain Specified Circumstances

Consider the following example:

If Sharon visits Vancouver, which one of the following must be true?

The answer choices are:

(A) *Hubert visits Montreal.*
(B) *Lori visits Montreal.*
(C) *Paul visits Montreal.*
(D) *Lori visits the same city as Paul.*
(E) *Lori visits the same city as Roberta.*

In order to answer this question, start with the supposition that Sharon visits Vancouver and then ask if anything follows from that. In fact, something does follow. Consider the first condition, which tells you that Sharon visits a different city than Paul. From these two pieces of information, you can conclude that Paul visits either Montreal or Toronto, but not Vancouver (because Sharon visits Vancouver and Paul cannot visit the same city that she does). This is your first result, and checking this result against the answer choices, you'll find that you can't answer the question yet. In particular, you don't know whether (C) has to be true. You've only determined that it **can** be true.

Next, note that Paul is not the only one who visits Montreal or Toronto, but not Vancouver. The third condition tells you that this is true of Lori as well. And from the discussion in "Figuring Out the Setup" on pages 6–7 you know that only two cities will be visited by any of the students. Vancouver is one of those cities, since you started with the supposition that Sharon visits Vancouver. You don't know whether the other city is Montreal or Toronto. But you do know that whichever it is, it has to be the city that both Paul and Lori visit, since neither of them visits Vancouver.

Checking this second result against the answer choices, you'll find that you're done. Your second result guarantees the truth of answer choice (D) ("Lori visits the same city as Paul"). There is no need to check the other answer choices. Nor is there any need to work out even a single complete acceptable outcome. The moral of the story is this: use your time wisely.

NOTE. A check of the incorrect answer choices, if one had been done, would have revealed a situation that is fairly typical in the case of questions about what must be true. Some of the answer choices—(B) and (C)—are things that can be true but don't have to be true, and some of them—(A) and (E)—are things that can't be true. Among the incorrect answer choices, you might encounter any combination of things that can't be true and things that can be true but don't have to be.

So what generally applicable strategies can be extracted from the way the question above was answered?

When approaching a question about what must be true under certain specified circumstances, the first thing to do is to see what inferences, if any, you can draw on the basis of the setup conditions and how they interact with the specified circumstances. Having drawn any immediately available inferences, check them against the answer choices. If, on the basis of those inferences, one of the answer choices has to be true, you're done. Remember that your objective is to select the correct answer and move on to the next question, not to prove that the incorrect answer choices are wrong.

If none of the immediately available inferences matches any of the answer choices, try to see what can be inferred from the inferences you've already made (in conjunction with the setup conditions). Check this second round of inferences against the answer choices. If any of these inferences match one of the answer choices, you're done. This is what happened in the example above. Keep doing this until you're done.

CAUTION. Suppositions that are introduced in individual questions are **never** carried over to other questions. For example, in the question discussed above, the supposition "if Sharon visits Vancouver" applies only to that question. Once you're done with the question, you shouldn't assume that Sharon visits Vancouver. The correct answer to that one question depended on the supposition, but in moving from one question to another, suppositions are not brought along. This is why it is possible for the suppositions in different questions to be inconsistent with each other.

When considering "what must be true," it's possible to rule out an incorrect answer choice by constructing an acceptable outcome in which that answer choice is not true. To see how this would work, consider the example above, which asks what must be true if Sharon visits Vancouver. Suppose you were trying to rule out (B) ("Lori visits Montreal") by constructing an acceptable outcome in which (B) is false. You'd start with the following partial diagram:

$$\underline{M} \qquad \underline{T} \qquad \underline{V}$$
$$ \qquad L \qquad S$$

The starting point for the question is that Sharon visits Vancouver, so you can go ahead and enter this in the diagram. Now, to have an outcome in which (B) is false, Lori has to visit either Toronto or Vancouver. But Lori visiting Vancouver is ruled out by the third condition, so if Lori doesn't visit Montreal, she must visit Toronto. Since you then have Lori visiting Toronto and Sharon visiting Vancouver, the city visited by none of the students must be Montreal. This is what's represented in the partial diagram above.

Continue by drawing further inferences from the conditions. From the first condition you can infer that Paul has to visit Toronto. So you can add Paul to the diagram as follows:

$$\underline{M} \qquad \underline{T} \qquad \underline{V}$$
$$ \qquad L, P \qquad S$$

From the second condition you know that Hubert and Roberta have to visit the same city. But that city can't be Toronto, because that would mean that only one person would visit Vancouver, contrary to the fifth condition. So Hubert and Roberta must visit Vancouver, along with Sharon. This gives you the following outcome:

$$\underline{M} \qquad \underline{T} \qquad \underline{V}$$
$$ \qquad L, P \qquad H, R, S$$

This is an outcome in which (B) is false but satisfies all the setup conditions plus the specific circumstance introduced in the question. So (B) does not have to be true and can thus be eliminated.

What Must Be True on the Basis of the Setup Conditions Alone

Not all of the questions that ask about what must be true ask what must be true under particular circumstances specified in the question. Some questions ask about what must be true merely on the basis of the setup.

An example of a question that asks about what must be true on the basis of the setup alone is the following:

Which one of the following must be true?

A correct answer would be:

Hubert visits a different city than Lori.

This follows directly from the setup conditions. Hubert cannot visit the same city as Lori, because if he did, that city would receive visits from four of the students: Hubert, Roberta (who, by the second condition, visits the same city as Hubert), Lori, and either Paul or Sharon (since only two cities get visited, and Paul and Sharon cannot visit the same city, on account of the first condition). But that would mean that only one student—either Paul or Sharon—would visit one of the cities, and the fifth condition would then be violated. So you know that Hubert must visit a different city than Lori.

Questions that ask about what must be true on the basis of the setup alone have an interesting property: you can add the correct answer to what you have already inferred from the setup. Something that must be true on the basis of the setup alone is nothing but a logical consequence of how the setup conditions interact. Of course, before you use this result to help you answer other questions, you want to be very sure that the answer you selected is indeed the correct one.

> **NOTE.** In addition to questions about what must be true, you may encounter questions such as the following:
>
> *Which one of the following must be false?*
> *Which one of the following CANNOT be true?*
> *Each of the following could be true EXCEPT:*
>
> In all of these cases, the correct answer is something that is not true in even a single acceptable outcome. So among the incorrect answer choices you will find things that must be true as well as things that could be true.

QUESTIONS THAT ASK ABOUT WHAT COULD BE TRUE

Many Analytical Reasoning questions ask about what could be true rather than about what must be true. Something that could be true is something that is true in at least one acceptable outcome, even if there are many acceptable outcomes in which it is false. This means that the incorrect answer choices are all things that **cannot** be true in any acceptable outcome.

As with questions about what must be true, some questions ask what could be true under certain specified circumstances; others ask what could be true on the basis of the setup alone.

What Could Be True Under Certain Specified Circumstances

Consider the following question:

If Roberta visits Toronto, which one of the following could be true?

The five answer choices are:

(A) *Lori visits Toronto.*
(B) *Lori visits Vancouver.*
(C) *Paul visits Toronto.*
(D) *Paul visits Vancouver.*
(E) *Sharon visits Vancouver.*

How do you approach a question like this? A first step is to quickly check to see if any of the answer choices can be immediately ruled out as being in direct violation of one of the setup conditions. In this case, you would rule out (B) as directly violating the third condition, which requires that Lori visit either Montreal or Toronto. (There's no need to methodically go through each condition to see if any of the answer choices violate one of the conditions. That's a good strategy for orientation questions, but not usually for other questions. For nonorientation questions that ask for what can be true, just give the answer choices a quick look to see if any of them obviously violate something in the setup.)

Next, turn to the circumstance specified in the question—in this case, that Roberta visits Toronto—and work from that. If Roberta visits Toronto, Hubert also visits Toronto, as required by the second condition. Since by the first condition Sharon visits a different city than Paul, either Sharon or Paul will also visit Toronto, because only two cities are visited by any of the students. Toronto will thus be visited by three of the students.

So which city will be visited by just two students, Montreal or Vancouver? Since one of those two students must be Lori, it has to be Montreal; it cannot be Vancouver, because of the third condition. This means that none of the students visits Vancouver. So the answer choices specifying a visit to Vancouver (that is, (B), (D), and (E)) cannot be true. That leaves you with (A) and (C). But since you also know that Lori visits Montreal, you know that (A) cannot be true. So you know that (C) has to be the correct answer.

The approach above is to start with the setup conditions and then turn to the specific circumstance specified in the question and see what can be inferred from it in conjunction with the setup conditions. The emphasis here is not on what can be inferred to be the case, but on what **cannot** be the case, because the goal is to eliminate the incorrect answer choices and find the one that could be true. All of the incorrect answer choices must be false.

It is also possible to arrive at the correct answer by a different method. Assume that the answer choices, each in turn, are true. In four of the five cases, this assumption will lead you into a contradiction, thereby showing that the answer choice cannot be true.

Using this method to answer the question above, you would start by assuming that (A) is true. That is, you would assume that Lori visits Toronto. So Toronto would be visited by both Lori and Roberta. By the second condition, if Roberta visits Toronto, so does Hubert. That means that the other city visited would be visited by Paul and Sharon. But the first condition rules this out. So under the circumstance specified by the question—that Roberta visits Toronto—Lori cannot visit Toronto.

Next you assume that (B) is true—namely, that Lori visits Vancouver. But this is immediately ruled out by the third condition.

You then assume that (C) is true—that Paul visits Toronto. So Toronto would be visited by Paul, Roberta (as specified in the question), and Hubert (as specified by the second condition). That leaves Sharon and Lori to visit Montreal. This outcome satisfies all of the setup conditions, and is thus acceptable. Thus you know that (C) could be true, and you're done.

What Could Be True on the Basis of the Setup Conditions Alone

An example of a question that asks about what could be true on the basis of the setup alone is the following:

Which one of the following could be true?

The answer choices are:

(A) *Hubert and Lori both visit Toronto.*
(B) *Paul and Sharon both visit Vancouver.*
(C) *Roberta and Sharon both visit Montreal.*
(D) *Hubert visits Toronto and Paul visits Vancouver.*
(E) *Roberta visits Montreal and Sharon visits Vancouver.*

The first step, as usual, is to check if any of the answer choices can be immediately ruled out as being in direct violation of one of the setup conditions. In this case, (B) can be eliminated on those grounds, because it is in direct violation of the first condition. In addition, (D) can be eliminated as being in violation of the fourth condition.

That leaves you with (A), (C), and (E). You will have to evaluate these three answer choices one by one to see which one cannot be eliminated.

So assume that (A) is true. If Hubert and Lori both visit Toronto, then by the second condition Roberta must visit Toronto as well. That leaves Paul and Sharon to visit a city together, which is ruled out by the first condition. So (A) cannot be true.

Assume, then, that (C) is true. If Roberta and Sharon both visit Montreal, then by the second condition Hubert must visit Montreal as well. That leaves Paul and Lori to visit a city together, and nothing prevents them from visiting Toronto. This outcome satisfies all of the setup conditions, and is thus acceptable. Thus you know that (C) could be true, and you're done. There is no need to evaluate (E).

NOTE. In addition to questions about what could be true, you may encounter questions such as the following:

Which one of the following could be false?
Each of the following must be true EXCEPT:

In both of these cases, the correct answer is something that is not true in at least one acceptable outcome. Thus, all of the incorrect answer choices will be things that must be true.

You might also encounter a question that asks:

Which one of the following could be, but need not be, true?

In a case like this, as in any question that asks what could be true, the correct answer is something that is true in at least one acceptable outcome. What's special in these cases is that both things that **must** be true and things that **cannot** be true are incorrect answer choices for this sort of question.

REPLACING A CONDITION WITH A SUBSTITUTE CONDITION

Sometimes you'll be asked to identify a condition that could replace one or two of the existing conditions in the setup without affecting the set of possible outcomes. Here's an example of such a question, along with answer choices:

Which one of the following, if substituted for the condition that Sharon visits a different city than Paul, would have the same effect in determining which of the students visit which of the cities?

(A) *Either Paul or Sharon, but not both, visits Montreal.*
(B) *Hubert visits a different city than Lori.*
(C) *Sharon visits a different city than Roberta.*
(D) *Paul visits the same city as Roberta.*
(E) *Exactly one other student visits the same city as Lori.*

In questions like these, you need to be sure that when you replace the original condition with the new one, the resulting possible outcomes are the same as the ones that were possible before the condition was replaced. This means not only that all of the original possibilities still remain, but also that no new possibilities are introduced.

So one strategy for answering this kind of question is to rule out the incorrect answer choices by asking two questions:

- Does the new condition rule out outcomes that the original condition allows?

- Does the new condition allow outcomes that the original condition does not?

If the answer to either of these questions is yes, then the new condition offered in the answer choice cannot be correct.

Let's use this strategy to tackle the example here. In the case of answer choice (A), first ask yourself whether the new condition ("Either Paul or Sharon, but not both, visits Montreal") rules out outcomes that the original condition allows. The answer is yes. One consequence of the condition in (A) is that an outcome in which Montreal is not visited is not allowed. However, the original condition does allow for such an outcome. For example, the following outcome satisfies all of the conditions in the original setup, including the condition that Sharon visits a different city than Paul:

$$\underline{M} \qquad \underline{T} \qquad \underline{V}$$
$$ \qquad L, P \qquad H, R, S$$

Answer choice (A), in contrast, would rule out this possibility, since the condition in (A) requires that either Paul or Sharon visit Montreal. Answer choice (A), therefore, cannot be correct: this condition would not allow all of the outcomes that the original condition does.

Notice that the particular outcome above also tells you that answer choices (C) and (D) must be incorrect. The condition in (C) ("Sharon visits a different city than Roberta") would not allow the outcome above, since it is an outcome in which Sharon and Roberta both visit Vancouver. The condition in (D) ("Paul visits the same city as Roberta") would not allow this outcome, since it is an outcome in which Paul and Roberta visit different cities. Thus, like answer choice (A), answer choices (C) and (D) each rule out an outcome that the original condition allows.

Let's look now at answer choice (B), which contains the new condition that Hubert visits a different city than Lori. Answer choice (B), like the original condition, would allow the outcome discussed above. And, in fact, answer choice (B) does not rule out any outcomes that the original condition allows, since it's true that in every outcome that was possible with the original condition, Hubert visits a

different city than Lori. So you must now ask the second question: does the new condition in (B) allow outcomes that the original condition does not? The answer to this question is yes. Unlike the original condition, the condition in (B) allows an outcome such as the following:

$$\underline{M} \qquad \underline{T} \qquad \underline{V}$$
$$L, P, S \qquad H, R$$

In this case, contrary to the original condition, Sharon visits the same city as Paul. Because the condition in (B) would allow an outcome that is not allowed by the original condition, answer choice (B) cannot be correct.

At this point, you've ruled out all but one answer choice. So you know that answer choice (E) ("Exactly one other student visits the same city as Lori") must be correct, and you're done. There's no need to verify that the new condition could replace the original condition with the same effect on the possible outcomes. However, it might be instructive to take a closer look at (E) here.

Suppose that the condition in (E) replaces the condition that Sharon and Paul visit different cities. If exactly one other student visits the same city as Lori, you know that Lori cannot visit the same city that Hubert and Roberta visit together. The only way for there to be exactly one student visiting the same city as Lori is for either Sharon or Paul to visit the same city as Lori, with the other visiting whichever city is visited by Hubert and Roberta. What this means is that Sharon and Paul must visit different cities, which is what the original condition required. There are also no new effects created by the condition that exactly one other student visits the same city as Lori. So the condition in (E) can be substituted for the condition that Sharon visits a different city than Paul, with no change in what the possible outcomes are. In other words, the condition in (E) rules out all of the outcomes that the original condition ruled out and it allows all of the outcomes that the original condition allowed.

CONDITIONAL STATEMENTS

Often one or more of the setup conditions is in the form of a conditional statement. Conditional statements that you're likely to encounter in Analytical Reasoning say that if something is the case, then something else is the case. For example, "If Theo is on the committee, then Vera is also on the committee." To work efficiently and effectively with Analytical Reasoning questions it is important to have a clear understanding of how to reason correctly with conditional statements and to know what errors to avoid.

CROSS-REFERENCE. The topic of conditional statements is discussed from a slightly different perspective in the section on "Necessary Conditions and Sufficient Conditions" in the Logical Reasoning guide on pages 29–30.

Conditional relationships ("conditionals") can be expressed in a variety of ways. The following are all equivalent ways of stating the same conditional:

(1) If Theo is on the committee, Vera is also on the committee.
(2) If Vera is not on the committee, Theo is not on the committee.
(3) Theo is not on the committee if Vera is not on the committee.
(4) Theo is not on the committee unless Vera is on the committee.
(5) Theo is on the committee only if Vera is on the committee.

All of these, despite the differences in their formulation, express exactly the same conditional relationship between Theo's being on the committee and Vera's being on the committee. What they all tell you is that Theo's being on the committee guarantees that Vera is on the committee. But none of them tells you that Vera's being on the committee guarantees that Theo is on the committee.

NOTE. The fact that all of the formulations displayed above are logically equivalent is not intuitively obvious. For most people, there is a marked difference in focus between some of these. For example, (1) seems to invite getting the facts about Theo straight first and if it turns out that Theo is on the committee, this tells you something about Vera. By contrast, (4) seems to invite finding out whether Vera is on the committee and if it turns out that she is not, this tells you that Theo is not on the committee either. Looking at things this way, it is easy to miss the underlying equivalence. But familiarity with, and automatic reliance on, this equivalence is crucial for dealing effectively with many Analytical Reasoning questions. So time that you spend now becoming thoroughly familiar with these equivalences is time well spent. Come test day, you'll be able to handle conditionals no matter how they're worded.

How does a conditional—regardless of how it happens to be formulated—work in drawing inferences? What are the kinds of additional information that, taken in conjunction with a conditional, yield proper inferences? Let's look at an example. Take the conditional "If Theo is on the committee, then Vera is on the committee." There are basically four cases to consider: (1) Theo is on the committee, (2) Theo is not on the committee, (3) Vera is on the committee, and (4) Vera is not on the committee. Each of these cases is discussed in turn below:

1. **Theo is on the committee.** If this is true, then given the conditional (in any of its formulations), it's guaranteed that Vera is also on the committee. The conditional says as much. This case is straightforward.

2. **Theo is not on the committee.** If this is true, you cannot use the conditional (regardless of how it is formulated) to derive any legitimate inferences about Vera. In particular, you **cannot** conclude that Vera is not on the committee. As far as the conditional goes, Theo's not being on the committee is consistent both with Vera's being on the committee and with her not being there. The conditional is simply silent about whether or not Vera is on the committee.

3. **Vera is on the committee.** If this is true, you cannot use the conditional (regardless of how it is formulated) to derive any legitimate inferences about Theo. In particular, you **cannot** conclude that Theo is also on the committee. In fact, this point was just made in the discussion of point 2 above. As was said there, Theo's not being on the committee is consistent with Vera's being on the committee. In the same way, Vera's being on the committee is consistent with Theo's not being on the committee.

4. **Vera is not on the committee.** If this is true, you can use the conditional (in any of its formulations) to derive a legitimate inference about Theo. You can infer that Theo is not on the committee either. This is because if Theo were on the committee without Vera also being on the committee, then the conditional, "If Theo is on the committee, Vera must also be on the committee," would be violated. So, to sum this up, if Vera is not on the committee, the only way not to violate the conditional is for Theo not to be on the committee either.

NOTE. Sometimes Analytical Reasoning questions call for inferences involving more than one conditional. Suppose you're given two conditionals like the following:

If Theo is on the committee, Vera is on the committee.

If Vera is on the committee, Ralph is on the committee.

From these you can legitimately infer

If Theo is on the committee, Ralph is on the committee.

and

If Ralph is not on the committee, Theo is not on the committee.

Note that these inferences can be derived no matter how the conditionals on which they are based are formulated. So, for example, from these versions:

If Vera is not on the committee, Theo is not on the committee.

Vera is not on the committee unless Ralph is on the committee.

you can make the same two inferences:

If Theo is on the committee, Ralph is on the committee.

and

If Ralph is not on the committee, Theo is not on the committee.

WORDINGS USED IN ANALYTICAL REASONING QUESTIONS

In Analytical Reasoning questions, the language used in presenting the setup and asking the questions must be precise and unambiguous. As a result, many things are spelled out at greater length and in more detail than they would be in most other kinds of writing. For example, in a setup that talks about a group of people who will give presentations at a meeting, it will probably be stated explicitly that each person makes only one presentation and that the people give their presentations one after another. Here are some other examples:

- **at some time before/immediately before**

These expressions typically occur in place of "before" alone. This is because if you were simply told, for example, that "Smith's presentation comes before Jeng's presentation," it might be unclear whether someone else's presentation could occur between them. And so it might not be clear whether some outcome is acceptable or not. The use of phrases like "immediately before" is intended to avoid such ambiguity.

If you're told, "Smith's presentation comes **immediately before** Jeng's presentation," you know that no other presentation can occur between those two. On the other hand, if you're told, "Smith's presentation comes **at some time before** Jeng's presentation," you know that another presentation can, but doesn't have to, occur between those two. If another presentation had to occur between Smith's and Jeng's presentations, this would have to be said explicitly.

Similarly, you may be told that Smith's office is on "a higher floor" than Jeng's office (which allows for the possibility that the two offices are on adjacent floors and for the possibility that they are on nonadjacent floors), or you may be told that Smith's office is on the floor "immediately above" Jeng's office (which ensures that there are no other floors between the ones on which Smith's office and Jeng's office are located).

Or you might be told that within a row of offices, Smith's office is "the office" between Jeng's office and Robertson's office. This would tell you something different than if you were told that Smith's office is "an office" between Jeng's office and Robertson's office. In the first case, the use of the definite article "the" indicates that there is only one office between Jeng's and Robertson's offices, namely, Smith's office. In the second case, however, it is left open whether there are any offices in addition to Smith's office between those of Jeng and Robertson.

- **at least/at most/exactly**

There are times when simply being told that there must be three people on a certain committee would leave you uncertain whether this means that there can be more than three people on the committee or that there must be exactly three people on the committee. This kind of uncertainty is avoided by using precise language to talk about numbers. If the point is that three is the minimum number of committee members, you would typically be told that there must be **at least** three people on the committee. If three is the maximum number of committee members, then typically you would be told that there must be **at most** three people on the committee. Otherwise, you would typically be told that there must be **exactly** three people on the committee.

- **respectively/not necessarily in that order**

If you were asked to evaluate whether the statement "If Y is performed first, the songs performed second, third, and fourth could be T, X, and O," you might wonder what is meant. Does this mean (1) T, X, and O in some order or other, or does it mean (2) T second, X third, and O fourth? In Analytical Reasoning questions, this potential uncertainty is avoided by using precise wording. If (1) is what is meant, you'll see wording like "If Y is performed first, the songs performed second, third, and fourth could be T, X, and O, **not necessarily in that order**." If (2) is what is meant, you'll see wording like "If Y is performed first, the songs performed second, third, and fourth could be T, X, and O, respectively."

MORE POINTS TO CONSIDER

Here are several points to keep in mind. Some have been mentioned earlier and some are additional notes and tips.

- Always keep in mind that your objective is to select the correct answer, not to produce a comprehensive account of all the logical possibilities available under the circumstances specified in the question. Arriving at the correct answer almost never requires working out all of the possible outcomes.

- As you draw inferences on the basis of how the question-specific circumstances interact with the setup conditions, keep checking the answer choices. At any point, you might be able to identify the correct answer. Or you might be able to eliminate some answer choices as incorrect. If you have succeeded in identifying the correct answer, you are done even if there are still further inferences you could draw or if there are some answer choices that you have not yet been able to eliminate. There is no need for you to prove that those answer choices are incorrect. By the same token, if you have succeeded in eliminating all but one answer choice, you are done even if you have not independently shown that the remaining answer choice is correct.

- Remember that when dealing with Analytical Reasoning questions, anything is acceptable that is not prohibited by the setup conditions or by what is implied by the setup conditions along with any circumstances specified in the question. Do not make any unwarranted assumptions, however natural they might seem. For example, if you are told that a committee must include an expert on finance and an expert on marketing, do not take it for granted that the committee's expert on finance must be a different person from the committee's expert on marketing.

- In Analytical Reasoning questions, careful and literal reading is of critical importance. Even though time management is important, it is even more important not to read too quickly. To give a specific example of the kind of problem that can arise, consider the following two statements: "F and G cannot both go on vacation during July" and "Neither F nor G can go on vacation during July." There are a number of superficial resemblances between them. However, the two are not equivalent, and mistaking one for the other would almost certainly lead to errors. If F goes on vacation in July and G does not, the first condition is not violated, but the second one is.

- Recall the earlier discussion of active elements in the setup that aren't mentioned in any of the conditions. It isn't necessary for all of the individual elements to be explicitly constrained by the setup conditions. If a particular element is not explicitly mentioned in the conditions, this means that the element is constrained only by what happens with the other elements. It does not mean that the set of setup conditions is incomplete or otherwise defective.

- Keep in mind that there can only be one correct answer among the answer choices, even though there might be many possible correct answers to the question. Suppose you are asked a question like, "Which one of the following must be advertised during week 2," based on a setup involving seven products to be advertised during a four-week period. Suppose further that you determine that product H must be advertised during week 2, but that H does not appear among the answer choices. Does this mean that the question is defective? No. In this case it could be that G is also a product that must be advertised during week 2, and G is one of the answer choices.

- Many questions ask you to identify an acceptable partial outcome. For example, the setup might be concerned with dividing a group of people into two teams, team 1 and team 2. The question might ask which one of the answer choices is an acceptable team 1. In a case like this, if you look for violations of setup conditions only within team 1, the team that actually appears in the answer choices, you might find more than one answer choice that seems acceptable. But remember that what has to be acceptable is an outcome as a whole—the composition of **both** team 1 and team 2. So, even though team 2 is not displayed in any of the answer choices, you still need to check it for violations of the setup conditions. That is, you would need to work out the outcome for team 2 for those answer choices that you cannot otherwise eliminate as incorrect.

- Recall the earlier discussion of what could or must be true on the basis of the setup conditions alone. It is extremely important that you keep in mind the point made there: circumstances specified in an individual question hold for that question only and never carry over to any other questions.

A GUIDE TO LOGICAL REASONING QUESTIONS

ARGUMENTS

What Is an Argument?
Most Logical Reasoning questions focus on arguments, which are sets of statements that present evidence and draw a conclusion on the basis of that evidence. These arguments are generally short and self-contained.

Consider this basic example:

Sarah is well qualified, and the hiring committee is very familiar with her work. Therefore, she will probably receive a job offer.

This is a simple argument. Two pieces of evidence are presented. These are the premises of the argument. These **premises** are offered in support of the view that Sarah will probably receive a job offer. This is the **conclusion** of the argument.

Let's look at a second case:

Computer Whiz is a well-respected magazine with a large readership, so its product endorsements carry a lot of weight in the computer electronics marketplace. The X2000 display monitor was recently endorsed by Computer Whiz. It is therefore likely that sales of the X2000 monitor will increase dramatically.

In this argument, information about the magazine's reputation and large readership serves as a basis for reaching an **intermediate**, or **subsidiary**, **conclusion**: that its endorsements are very influential in the marketplace. This intermediate conclusion in conjunction with a premise that reports that the X2000 was recently endorsed by the magazine provides the grounds for the prediction of an increase in sales. This prediction is the **main**, **or overall**, **conclusion** of the argument.

Identifying the Parts of an Argument
An argument can be analyzed by identifying its various parts and the roles that those parts play. The most basic parts of an argument are premises and conclusions. As we have already seen, an argument may have one or more intermediate conclusions in addition to its overall conclusion.

Premises come in a variety of forms. Some premises are specific matters of fact, some are definitions, and others are broad principles or generalizations. What all premises

have in common is that they are put forward as true without support. That is, there is no attempt within the argument to prove or justify them. In contrast, a conclusion is **not** simply asserted. A conclusion is presented as being justified by certain premises. Thus, the conclusion of an argument is open to the challenge that it is not adequately supported by the premises. (Premises, of course, can also be challenged, on grounds such as factual accuracy, but such challenges are not matters of logic.)

One thing to remember about premises and conclusions is that they can come in any order. Premises are presented in support of a conclusion, but this does not mean that premises always precede the conclusion. A conclusion may be at the beginning, middle, or end of an argument. Consider the following examples:

Dolores is far more skillful than Victor is at securing the kind of financial support the Volunteers for Literacy Program needs, and Dolores does not have Victor's propensity for alienating the program's most dedicated volunteers. Therefore, the Volunteers for Literacy Program would benefit if Dolores took Victor's place as director.

Dolores is far more skillful than Victor is at securing the kind of financial support the Volunteers for Literacy Program needs. Therefore, the program would benefit if Dolores took Victor's place as director, especially since Dolores does not have Victor's propensity for alienating the program's most dedicated volunteers.

The Volunteers for Literacy Program would benefit if Dolores takes Victor's place as director, since Dolores is far more skillful than Victor is at securing the kind of financial support the program needs and Dolores does not have Victor's propensity for alienating the program's most dedicated volunteers.[1]

These three examples all present the same argument. In each example, the conclusion is that the Volunteers for Literacy Program would benefit if Dolores took Victor's place as director, and this conclusion is supported by the same two premises. But each example expresses the argument in a different way, with the conclusion appearing in the final, middle, and initial position, respectively. It is important, then, to focus on the role each statement plays in the argument as a whole. Position within the argument simply doesn't matter.

 [1]See Appendix B, page 83.

Another thing to keep in mind is the presence of indicator words that mark the roles that statements play in arguments. For example, "therefore" often precedes a conclusion; it is a common conclusion indicator. So are "thus," "hence," "consequently," "it follows that," "it can be concluded that," and various others. Similarly, premises are often preceded by indicator words, the most typical being "since" and "because." However, do not rely uncritically on these indicator words. They can be misleading, especially in the case of complex arguments, which might contain one or more subarguments. There is no completely mechanical way of identifying the roles that various statements play within an argument.

It is worth noting that people, in making arguments, often do not confine themselves to presenting just the conclusion and the statements that support it. Likewise, the short arguments in Logical Reasoning questions often include statements that are neither premises nor conclusions. This includes statements that indicate the motivation for making the argument, statements that convey background information, and statements that identify the position the argument comes out against. So don't assume that everything that is not part of the argument's conclusion must be functioning as support for that conclusion.

How the Argument Goes

Once you have identified the premises and the conclusion, the next step is to get clear about exactly how the argument is meant to go; that is, how the grounds offered for the conclusion are actually supposed to bear on the conclusion. Understanding how an argument goes is a crucial step in answering many questions that appear on the LSAT. This includes questions that ask you to identify a reasoning technique used within an argument, questions that require you to match the pattern of reasoning used in two separate arguments, and a variety of other question types.

Determining how an argument goes involves discerning how the premises are supposed to support the overall conclusion. Consider, for example, the argument presented earlier about the Volunteers for Literacy Program, which concludes that the program would benefit if Dolores took Victor's place as director. Two considerations in support of this conclusion are offered: one asserting Dolores's superiority in securing financial support and the other charging that Victor is more prone to alienating dedicated volunteers. These two considerations are both relevant to the conclusion, since (all other things being equal) a program benefits from having a director who is both better at fund-raising and less likely to alienate volunteers. Each of these

considerations provides some support for the conclusion, and the support provided by one is completely independent of the support provided by the other.

In other arguments, the way in which premises support a conclusion can be much more complex. Consider this example:

The years 1917, 1937, 1956, 1968, 1979, and 1990 are all notable for the occurrence of both popular uprisings and near-maximum sunspot activity. During heavy sunspot activity, there is a sharp rise in positively charged ions in the air people breathe, and positively charged ions are known to make people anxious and irritable. Therefore, it is likely that sunspot activity has actually been a factor in triggering popular uprisings.[2]

The conclusion of this argument, signaled by "Therefore," is that it is likely that sunspot activity has been a factor in triggering popular uprisings. There are three premises. The first tells us about specific years in which both heavy sunspot activity and popular uprisings occurred. The other two are generalizations: that there is a sharp rise in positively charged ions in the air during heavy sunspot activity, and that positively charged ions make people anxious and irritable.

So how does this argument go? The first premise provides some direct support for the conclusion, but this support is very weak, circumstantial evidence. The second and third premises do not support the conclusion directly, but only in conjunction with each other. If these two premises are true, they work together to establish that sunspots are a causal factor in increased irritability. Notice that there is still no link between sunspots and popular uprisings. There is some plausibility, however, to the idea that increased irritability makes popular uprisings more likely, and the argument tacitly assumes that this is in fact so.

If we make this assumption then, we can see the connection between sunspot activity and popular uprisings. This greatly enhances the evidence that the first premise provides.

CROSS-REFERENCE. You can learn more about the role of assumptions in arguments in the discussion on pages 33–37 in the "Assumptions" section.

Questions About How the Argument Goes

Your test may include questions that ask you about how an argument proceeds overall, or about the logical role played by a particular part of an argument, or about the logical move one participant in a dialogue makes in responding to the other. Understanding how the relevant argument goes puts you in a position to answer these questions. Three examples are briefly discussed below.

EXAMPLE 1

Red squirrels are known to make holes in the bark of sugar maple trees and to consume the trees' sap. Since sugar maple sap is essentially water with a small concentration of sugar, the squirrels almost certainly are after either water or sugar. Water is easily available from other sources in places where maple trees grow, so the squirrels would not go to the trouble of chewing holes in trees just to get water. Therefore, they are probably after the sugar.[3]

The question based on this argument is simply:

The argument proceeds by

The conclusion of this argument is quite easy to identify: red squirrels, in making holes in the bark of sugar maple trees, are probably after the sugar contained in the trees' sap. The argument arrives at this conclusion by first noting that since maple tree sap is essentially just water and sugar, the squirrels must be after either the one or the other. The argument goes on to reject the idea that it is the water that the squirrels are after, on the grounds that water is readily available for less effort where maple trees grow.

Once you have figured out how the argument goes, you're ready to check the answer choices to find the best characterization of the argument's reasoning. In this particular case, the best characterization is:

rejecting a possible alternative explanation for an observed phenomenon

This is not the only way to describe how the argument proceeds, and it may not be the description you would have given. But it is an accurate characterization and is thus the correct answer. So keep in mind when checking the answer choices that the correct answer may be just one of several acceptable ways of putting things.

EXAMPLE 2

In order to determine automobile insurance premiums for a driver, insurance companies calculate various risk factors; as the risk factors increase, so does the premium. Certain factors, such as the driver's age and past accident history, play an important role in these calculations. Yet these premiums should also increase with the frequency with which a person drives. After all, a person's chance of being involved in a mishap increases in proportion to the number of times that person drives.[4]

The question based on this argument is:

The claim that insurance premiums should increase as the frequency with which a driver drives increases plays which one of the following roles in the argument?

The first step in determining how this argument goes is identifying the conclusion. To do this, find the position for which the argument offers support.

The short phrase "after all" at the beginning of the fourth sentence indicates that the statement that follows functions as a premise. This premise essentially says that the frequency with which a person drives is a factor in their risk of being involved in a traffic accident. We know from the first sentence that risk factors matter in determining a driver's automobile insurance premiums: as certain risk factors increase, the premium increases. Putting all of this together, we see that the argument is constructed to support the position stated in the third sentence: "…these premiums should also increase with the frequency with which the person drives."

So the claim that insurance premiums should increase as the frequency with which a driver drives increases is the conclusion of the argument. That is its role in the argument. The answer choice that expresses this, in some way or other, is the correct one.

[3]See Appendix B, page 84.
[4]See Appendix B, page 84.

EXAMPLE 3

Zachary: The term "fresco" refers to paint that has been applied to wet plaster. Once dried, a fresco indelibly preserves the paint that a painter has applied in this way. Unfortunately, additions known to have been made by later painters have obscured the original fresco work done by Michelangelo in the Sistine Chapel. Therefore, in order to restore Michelangelo's Sistine Chapel paintings to the appearance that Michelangelo intended them to have, everything except the original fresco work must be stripped away.

Stephen: But it was extremely common for painters of Michelangelo's era to add painted details to their own fresco work after the frescoes had dried.[5]

The corresponding question is:

Stephen's response to Zachary proceeds by

Zachary tells us that Michelangelo's frescoes in the Sistine Chapel had additions made to them by later painters. On the basis of this he argues that everything except Michelangelo's original fresco work has to be stripped away if the paintings are to have the appearance Michelangelo intended them to have.

Stephen's response makes clear that for painters of Michelangelo's era, the frescoes as originally executed did not necessarily have the appearance that those painters intended them to have. So Stephen's response points to and casts doubt on an assumption of Zachary's argument. This assumption is that Michelangelo did not make additions to his own fresco work in order to give the paintings the appearance that he wanted them to have.

Turning to the answer choices, you find this statement among them:

calling into question an assumption on which Zachary's conclusion depends

This statement correctly characterizes how Stephen's response to Zachary proceeds.

A Point to Consider

- Arguments vary widely in their strength, that is, in the extent to which their conclusions are justified by their premises. In the extreme case—the case of a "deductively valid" (that is, conclusive) argument—the truth of the conclusion is completely guaranteed by the truth of the premises. In other words, anyone who accepts those premises is thereby committed to accepting the conclusion. In most cases, however, the relationship of the premises to the conclusion is less strict: the premises provide some grounds for accepting the conclusion, but these grounds are not airtight. In other words, someone might accept all of the premises of such an argument yet still be logically justified in not accepting its conclusion.

Identifying the Main Conclusion of an Argument

Some questions present you with an argument and ask you to identify its main conclusion. In questions of this kind, the conclusion is actually drawn in the argument, but it is often stated somewhat indirectly and it is sometimes not signaled by any of the standard conclusion-indicator words such as "therefore" or "thus." To identify the conclusion, therefore, you also need to look at what the statements in the argument mean, and how they are related to each other. Look for a position that the argument as a whole is trying to establish, and rule out any statements that, either directly or indirectly, give reasons for that position. You should also eliminate statements that merely establish a context or supply background information.

AN EXAMPLE

Journalist: Obviously, though some animals are purely carnivorous, none would survive without plants. But the dependence is mutual. Many plant species would never have come to be had there been no animals to pollinate, fertilize, and broadcast their seeds. Also, plants' photosynthetic activity would deplete the carbon dioxide in Earth's atmosphere were it not constantly being replenished by the exhalation of animals, engine fumes, and smoke from fires, many set by human beings.[6]

The question asks:

Which one of the following most accurately expresses the main conclusion of the journalist's argument?

So, how do you tackle this question? First, read the argument through. You might immediately recognize that the argument is of a familiar sort. The argument is directed toward a position that has two sides to it: a very straightforward one that is simply asserted and a less obvious one that the argument goes to some trouble to establish. The first sentence presents the straightforward side of the position being argued for. The second sentence states the entire position. The third and fourth sentences make the case for the less obvious side of the position.

Suppose that after reading the argument you are not sure exactly how it goes. What do you do then? It might be helpful to go through the argument statement by statement and ask about each statement in turn, "Does this statement receive support from some other statement?" If so, the statement is either a subsidiary conclusion drawn to support the main conclusion or it is itself the main conclusion. If the statement does not receive support from anything else in the argument, ask whether it provides support for some other statement. If it does, it's a premise of the argument, and whatever statement it provides support for is either the main conclusion or a subsidiary conclusion.

In the journalist's argument, the first statement does not receive support from anything else that is said in the argument. It does, however, provide support for the second statement by establishing one side of the dependence that the second statement refers to. So the second statement is a candidate for being the main conclusion of the argument. If you go on to analyze the third and fourth statements, you'll find that neither receives any support from anything else in the argument and that each independently supports the second statement by establishing the other side of the mutual dependence. Since everything else in the argument goes toward supporting the second statement, it is clear that the second statement expresses the main conclusion of the argument.

The second statement states the main conclusion in a somewhat abbreviated way in that it doesn't spell out what is meant by "dependence." But having worked through the argument, we can recognize that the following is an accurate statement of the conclusion:

Just as animals are dependent on plants for their survival, plants are dependent on animals for theirs.

The incorrect answer choices often restate a premise or part of a premise. For example, the following incorrect answer is a partial (and inaccurate) restatement of the fourth sentence of the journalist's argument:

Human activity is part of what prevents plants from depleting the oxygen in Earth's atmosphere on which plants and animals alike depend.

Other incorrect answer choices may state something that can be inferred from statements in the argument but that is not the argument's main conclusion. Here is an example of this, based on the journalist's argument:

The chemical composition of Earth and its atmosphere depends, at least to some extent, on the existence and activities of the animals that populate Earth.

Some Points to Consider

- If there is a "thus" or "therefore" in the argument, do not assume that these words introduce the main conclusion of the argument. They often indicate a subsidiary conclusion rather than the main conclusion.

- With questions that ask you to identify the main conclusion, it is generally possible to form a fairly precise idea of what the correct answer will be like before considering the answer choices. Doing so makes it possible to select the correct answer very efficiently. You should also try to get a precise idea of the main conclusion, because some of the incorrect answer choices may be only slightly inaccurate. For example, if the actual conclusion is that something is likely to be true, an incorrect answer choice may say that it is definitely true. This choice is incorrect because it goes beyond the actual conclusion.

Matching Patterns of Reasoning in Arguments

There is another kind of question that tests your ability to determine how an argument goes. It begins with an argument and then asks you to choose one argument from among the answer choices that is most similar in its reasoning to the initial (or reference) argument. The questions themselves are worded in a variety of ways, including:

The pattern of reasoning in which of the following arguments is most similar to that in the argument above?

Which one of the following arguments is most similar in its reasoning to the argument above?

You don't need to come up with a verbal description of the pattern of reasoning in order to answer these questions. All you need is a solid intuitive grasp of the logical structure of the reference argument: what its conclusion is and how the premises fit together to support the conclusion.

These questions are asking for a match in logical structure, that is, the way the premises fit together to support the conclusion. So do not pay any attention to similarity or dissimilarity in subject matter, or to background material that is not part of the premises or the conclusion. Nor should you concern yourself with anything about the particular way the argument is laid out, such as the order in which the premises and the conclusion are presented.

AN EXAMPLE

All known deposits of the mineral tanzanite are in Tanzania. Therefore, because Ashley collects only tanzanite stones, she is unlikely ever to collect a stone not originally from Tanzania.[7]

The question asks:

Which one of the following is most similar in its reasoning to the argument above?

So what is the structure of the reasoning in the reference argument? There are two premises, the one about tanzanite deposits and the one about Ashley's collecting habits. And there is a conclusion: Ashley is unlikely ever to collect a stone not originally from Tanzania. Note that the conclusion merely says that something is unlikely, not that it will definitely not happen. The conclusion is probably qualified in this way because the premise about tanzanite deposits speaks only about the known deposits of that mineral, thereby leaving open the possibility that there are undiscovered tanzanite deposits outside of Tanzania.

But also note that the argument is a fairly strong one. The premises give a reasonable basis for accepting the conclusion: if the premises are true, the only way in which Ashley would ever collect a stone that is not originally from Tanzania is if tanzanite is someday discovered outside of Tanzania or if she begins to collect some different type of stone in the future.

The next step is to check the answer choices and to find the one with the same pattern of reasoning.

So let's try this answer choice:

Frogs are the only animals known to live in the lagoon on Scrag Island. The diet of the owls on Scrag Island consists of nothing but frogs from the island. Therefore, the owls are unlikely ever to eat an animal that lives outside the lagoon.

Does this follow the same pattern of reasoning as the argument about tanzanite? The conclusion has the right shape: it says that something is unlikely ever to happen, just as the conclusion of the reference argument does. In addition, this argument, like the reference argument, has a premise that limits itself to speaking about what is known to be true, thereby leaving open the possibility of cases unlike those now known. Plus, the second premise is exclusionary in nature: where the reference argument uses "only," this argument says "nothing but." So there are a number of resemblances between important parts of the two arguments.

However, whereas the reference argument is fairly strong, this argument is seriously flawed. Notice that the two premises do not rule out the possibility there are frogs on Scrag Island that do not live in the lagoon. So there seems to be a strong possibility that the owls on Scrag Island eat frogs that aren't from the lagoon. The conclusion of this argument thus receives little or no support from the premises. If the reasoning in this argument were closely parallel to that in the reference argument, its premises would provide similarly strong support for its conclusion. So this answer choice cannot be correct.

Let's try another one of the answer choices:

The only frogs yet discovered on Scrag Island live in the lagoon. The diet of all the owls on Scrag Island consists entirely of frogs on the island, so the owls will probably never eat an animal that lives outside the lagoon.

Here, too, the conclusion has the right shape: it says that something is unlikely ever to happen. In addition, this argument has a premise that limits itself to speaking about what is known to be the case. Plus, the second premise is exclusionary in nature.

In this case, the premises provide support for the conclusion in just the same way that the premises in the reference argument do for the conclusion of that argument. This argument can be paraphrased in a way that is parallel to the reference argument: All known frogs on Scrag Island live in the lagoon. Scrag Island owls eat only frogs. It is therefore unlikely that an owl on Scrag Island will ever eat an animal that does not live in the lagoon. Thus, the pattern of reasoning in the two arguments is essentially the same.

WHAT CAN BE CONCLUDED FROM THE INFORMATION PROVIDED

Many Logical Reasoning questions test your ability to determine what is supported by a body of available evidence. These questions ask you to pick one statement that can in some way or another be inferred from the available evidence. So, in effect, you are asked to distinguish between positions that are supported by the information that you have been given and positions that are not supported by that information. These questions come in a variety of forms.

Identifying a Position That Is Conclusively Established by Information Provided

Some questions test your ability to identify what follows logically from certain evidence or information. For these questions, you will be presented with information that provides **conclusive** support for one of the answer choices. Typical wordings for these questions include:

If the statements above are true, which one of the following must also be true?

Which one of the following logically follows from the statements above?

With these questions, you are looking for something that is **guaranteed** to be true by the information you have been given. That is, the correct answer will be a statement that **must** be true if the given information is true. Incorrect answer choices may receive some support from the information, but that support will be inconclusive. In other words, an incorrect answer choice could be false even if the information provided is true.

AN EXAMPLE

Any sale item that is purchased can be returned for store credit but not for a refund of the purchase price. Every home appliance and every piece of gardening equipment is on sale along with selected construction tools.[8]

The question asks:

If the statements above are true, which one of the following must also be true?

Notice that the statements have a common element: they talk about sale items. This common element allows you to combine bits of information to draw conclusions. For example, since all home appliances are sale items, you could conclude that any home appliance that is purchased can be returned for store credit. Because several conclusions like this can be drawn from these statements, you cannot determine the correct answer without reading the answer choices. So you need to go through the answer choices to find one that must be true if the statements are true.

One choice reads:

No piece of gardening equipment is returnable for a refund.

We are told that every piece of gardening equipment is a sale item and sale items are **not** returnable for a refund. So it must be true that gardening equipment is not returnable for a refund. This is the correct answer choice.

For the sake of comparison, consider another answer choice:

Some construction tools are not returnable for store credit.

To rule out this answer choice, you need to see that it does not have to be true if the statements in the passage are true. It obviously doesn't have to be true for construction tools that are on sale—the statements guarantee that those construction tools are returnable for store credit. As for the rest of the construction tools—those that aren't on sale—nothing indicates that they are not returnable for store credit. Based on what the statements say, it is possible, and even likely, that these tools are returnable for store credit. The answer choice is therefore incorrect.

In this example, you were given a set of statements that do not seem to be designed to lead to any particular conclusion. It was up to you to determine the implications of those statements. In other cases, however, the information may appear to be designed to lead you to a specific unstated conclusion. In such cases, the correct answer could be the unstated conclusion, if it logically follows from the information provided, or it could be some other statement that logically follows from that information.

Some Points to Consider

- For some claim to logically follow from certain information, that information has to guarantee that the claim is true. It isn't enough for the information to strongly support the claim; it has to conclusively establish the claim.

- Incorrect answers to questions about what logically follows can be claims that receive some support from the information but that nevertheless **could** be false even though all of the information is correct.

- Answer choices are often incorrect because they take things one step beyond what the evidence supports. They might make claims that are too sweeping; for example, they might say "all" when the evidence supports only a "most" statement. Or where a statement about what "is likely to be" is warranted, an incorrect answer choice might say "is." Or where a statement about "all known cases" is warranted, an incorrect answer choice might say "all cases."

- Remember that a modest or limited claim can be a correct answer even if the information also supports a stronger claim. If the information supports drawing the conclusion that there will be a festival in every month, then it also supports the conclusion that there will be a festival in June.

Identifying a Position Supported by Information Provided

Some questions ask you to identify a position that is supported by a body of evidence, but not supported conclusively. These questions might be worded as follows:

Which one of the following is most strongly supported by the information above?

Which one of the following can most reasonably be concluded on the basis of the information above?

The statements above, if true, most strongly support which one of the following?

For these questions, you will generally not be presented with an argument, but merely with some pieces of information. Your task is to evaluate that information and distinguish between the answer choice that receives strong support from that information (the correct answer) and answer choices that receive no significant support (the incorrect answer choices).

AN EXAMPLE
Consider the following pieces of information:

People should avoid taking the antacid calcium carbonate in doses larger than half a gram, for despite its capacity to neutralize stomach acids, calcium carbonate can increase the calcium level in the blood and thus impair kidney function. Moreover, just half a gram of it can stimulate the production of gastrin, a stomach hormone that triggers acid secretion.[9]

You are asked:

Which one of the following is most strongly supported by the information above?

With questions of this kind, you shouldn't expect the correct answer to follow in a strictly logical sense from the information, but you should expect the information to provide a strong justification for the correct answer. When you begin work on a question of this sort, you should note any obvious interconnections among the facts given, but there is no point in formulating a precise prediction of what the correct answer will look like. A sensible approach is to read the passage carefully, and make a mental note of any implications that you spot. Then go on to consider each answer choice in turn and determine whether that answer choice gets any support from the information you have been given.

Let's follow this approach with the question above. Reading the passage, you find that a certain antacid is described as having the obvious intended effect of neutralizing stomach acid but as also having adverse side effects if the dosage is too high. One of these adverse effects results in impaired kidney function and the other results in acid secretion in the stomach.

There is a suggestion in the passage that doses exceeding half a gram are necessary for the first effect to be triggered to any serious extent. The passage also suggests that doses of half a gram or more will trigger the second effect. No other implications of this passage stand out. At this point, it is probably a good idea to consider each answer choice in turn.

One answer choice is:

Doses of calcium carbonate smaller than half a gram can reduce stomach acid more effectively than much larger doses do.

Is this choice supported by the information? The passage does give reasons as to why this might be true. It tells us that doses of half a gram or more can stimulate the production of a stomach hormone that triggers acid secretion. This hormone might counteract any extra acid-neutralization that comes from additional calcium carbonate over and above a half-gram dose; but then again it might not. Perhaps the extra calcium carbonate neutralizes more stomach acid than it triggers. For this reason, this answer choice is not strongly supported by the information.

Another answer choice is:

Half a gram of calcium carbonate can causally contribute to both the secretion and the neutralization of stomach acids.

Is there support for this choice in the information provided? We have noted that at half a gram the secretion of acid in the stomach is triggered. The passage mentions the drug's "capacity to neutralize stomach acids," strongly suggesting that some acid-neutralizing effect occurs at any dosage level. So there is strong support in the passage for both parts of this answer choice.

Some Points to Consider

- In answering questions dealing with support for conclusions, base your judgment about whether or not a particular answer choice is supported strictly on the information that is explicitly provided in the passage. If the passage concerns a subject matter with which you are familiar, ignore any information you might have about the subject that goes beyond what you have been told.

- Keep in mind that the support for the correct answer does not have to involve all of the information provided. For instance, in the example about calcium carbonate, an adverse effect on the kidneys is mentioned, but this information plays no role in the support for the correct answer.

Identifying Points on Which Disputants Hold Conflicting Views

You may also encounter questions involving two speakers where the first speaker puts forward a position and the second responds to that position. You will then be asked something like:

The main point at issue between Sarah and Paul is whether

Which one of the following most accurately expresses the point at issue between Juan and Michiko?

On the basis of their statements, Winchell and Trent are committed to disagreeing over whether

AN EXAMPLE

Mary: Computers will make more information available to ordinary people than was ever available before, thus making it easier for them to acquire knowledge without consulting experts.

Joyce: As more knowledge became available in previous centuries, the need for specialists to synthesize and explain it to nonspecialists increased. So computers will probably create a greater dependency on experts.[10]

The question asks:

The dialogue most strongly supports the claim that Mary and Joyce disagree with each other about whether

In answering questions of this kind, you may find it useful to read the dialogue closely enough to form a clear mental picture of each person's stance and then go on to the answer choices.

Now consider this answer choice:

computers will make more information available to ordinary people

Does what Joyce and Mary say show that they disagree about this? Mary straightforwardly says that computers will make more information available to ordinary people. But what about Joyce? She predicts that computers will create a greater dependency on experts because of a historical trend of an increasing dependency on experts whenever more knowledge becomes available to ordinary people. She seems to assume that computers will make more information available to ordinary people, so she probably agrees with Mary on this point.

Now consider a second answer choice:

dependency on computers will increase with the increase of knowledge

Nothing either Mary or Joyce says commits either of them to a particular view on this position. This is because neither of them explicitly discusses the issue of people's dependency on computers. But there is certainly no indication at all that they hold opposing views on whether dependency on computers will increase with the increase of knowledge.

Finally, consider a third answer choice:

computers will increase the need for ordinary people seeking knowledge to turn to experts

Based on what she says, Mary straightforwardly disagrees with this claim. Computers, she says, will make it easier for ordinary people to acquire knowledge without consulting experts. Joyce, on the other hand, concludes that computers will create a greater dependency on experts. The precedent from past centuries that she cites in support of this conclusion makes it clear that nonspecialists—that is, ordinary people—will depend more on experts when knowledge increases. So Mary and Joyce disagree on whether the need for ordinary people to turn to experts will be increased by computers.

Some Points to Consider

- The evidence that two speakers disagree about a particular point always comes from what they explicitly say. Sometimes there is a direct conflict between something that one of the speakers says and something that the other speaker says. The phrasing of the question indicates that you should be looking for a direct conflict when it says something straightforward like "Max and Nina disagree over whether… " At other times the point of disagreement must be inferred from the explicit positions that the speakers take. The phrasing of the question will indicate that this inference needs to be made. For example, a question like "The dialogue provides the most support for the claim that Nikisha and Helen disagree over whether. . ." does not suggest that they disagree explicitly, only that there is some evidence that they disagree.

- Do not try to derive a speaker's likely position on a topic from a psychological stereotype. It may be true that a speaker who takes a certain position would be the kind of person who would likely hold certain other positions as well, but you should not rely on this sort of association. Rely only on what a speaker explicitly says and on what can be properly inferred from that.

- The incorrect answer choices are not necessarily positions that the two speakers can be shown to agree on. In many cases, the views of at least one of the speakers on a given position cannot be determined from what has been said.

Necessary Conditions and Sufficient Conditions

Suppose you read the following statements:

You don't deserve praise for something unless you did it deliberately.

Tom deliberately left the door unlocked.

Does it follow from these statements that Tom deserves praise for leaving the door unlocked? You can probably see that this doesn't follow. The first statement says that you have to do something deliberately in order to deserve praise for doing it. It doesn't say that any time you do something deliberately you thereby deserve praise for doing it. So the mere fact that Tom did something deliberately is not enough to bring us to the conclusion that Tom deserves praise for doing it.

To put it in a slightly more technical way, the first statement expresses a **necessary condition**. Doing something deliberately is a necessary condition for deserving praise for doing it. In Logical Reasoning questions, it can be very important to recognize whether something expresses a necessary condition or whether it expresses what is called a **sufficient condition**. If the first statement had said "If you do something deliberately then you deserve praise for doing it," it would be saying that doing something deliberately is a sufficient condition for deserving praise for doing it.

CROSS-REFERENCE. Reasoning involving necessary and sufficient conditions is also covered, from a slightly different perspective, in the "Conditional Statements" section of the Analytical Reasoning guide on pages 15–17.

In the example above, it is fairly easy to see that the first statement expresses a necessary condition but not a sufficient condition. This may be because it would be quite strange to say that doing something deliberately is a sufficient condition for deserving praise. That would imply that you deserve praise for anything you do deliberately, even if it is an immoral or criminal act. But the content of a statement doesn't always help you determine whether it expresses a necessary condition or a sufficient condition.

For this reason, it pays to devote very close attention to the precise wording of any statements that express conditions. And it pays to have a clear idea in your mind about how statements that express necessary conditions function in arguments and about how statements that express sufficient conditions function in arguments.

There are many ways to express a necessary condition. The necessary condition above could have been stated just as accurately in several different ways, including:

You deserve praise for something only if you did it deliberately.

You don't deserve praise for something if you didn't do it deliberately.

To deserve praise for something, you must have done it deliberately.

If you think carefully about these statements, you should see that they all mean the same thing. And you can see that none of them says that doing something deliberately is a sufficient condition for deserving praise.

Sufficient conditions can also be expressed in several different ways:

If it rains, the sidewalks get wet.

Rain is all it takes to get the sidewalks wet.

The sidewalks get wet whenever it rains.

These statements each tell us that rain is a sufficient condition for the sidewalks getting wet. It is sufficient, because rain is all that it takes to make the sidewalks wet. But notice that these statements do not say that rain is the only thing that makes the sidewalks wet. They do not rule out the possibility that the sidewalks can get wet from melting snow or from being sprayed with a garden hose. So these statements do not express necessary conditions for wet sidewalks, only sufficient conditions.

How Necessary Conditions Work in Inferences

We've already noted one thing about basing inferences on statements that express necessary conditions, such as

N: You deserve praise for something only if you did it deliberately.

If we are also given a case that satisfies the necessary condition, such as

Tom deliberately left the door unlocked

we cannot legitimately draw an inference. Specifically, the conclusion that Tom deserves praise for leaving the door unlocked does not follow.

Statements that express necessary conditions can play a part in legitimate inferences, of course, but only in combination with the right sort of information. Suppose that in addition to statement N we are told

Tom deserves praise for leaving the door unlocked.

This allows us to conclude that Tom deliberately left the door unlocked. Since statement N says that you have to do something deliberately in order to deserve praise for doing it, Tom must have deliberately left the door unlocked if he deserves praise for what he did.

Or, suppose that in addition to statement N we are told

Tom did not leave the door unlocked deliberately.

This allows us to conclude that Tom does not deserve praise for leaving the door unlocked. This follows because statement N insists that only deliberate actions deserve praise, and because we are told clearly that Tom's action is not deliberate.

So in general, when you have a statement that expresses a necessary condition, it allows you to infer something in just two cases: (1) you can infer from knowing that the necessary condition is **not** met that the thing it is the necessary condition for does **not** occur; (2) you can infer that the necessary condition is met from knowing that the thing it is the necessary condition for occurs.

How Sufficient Conditions Work in Inferences

Statements that express sufficient conditions can also serve as a basis for inferences. Let's revisit one of the earlier statements of a sufficient condition:

S: If it rains, the sidewalks get wet.

If we are told that the sufficient condition is satisfied (that is, we are told that it is raining), then we can legitimately draw the inference that the sidewalks are getting wet. This should be quite obvious.

We can also draw another conclusion from a statement of a sufficient condition, provided that we have the right sort of additional information. Suppose that in addition to statement S we are told that the sidewalks did not get wet. Since the sidewalks get wet whenever it rains, we can conclude with complete confidence that it didn't rain.

So in general, when you have a statement that expresses a sufficient condition, it allows you to infer something in just two cases: (1) if you know that the sufficient condition is met, then you can infer that the thing it is the sufficient condition for occurs; (2) you can infer that the sufficient condition is **not** met from knowing that the thing it is the sufficient condition for does **not** occur.

Though it may sometimes seem that there are other ways to draw an inference from a statement of a sufficient condition, there are none. Suppose that in addition to statement S, we are told that the sidewalks are wet. Can we legitimately conclude that it rained? No, because statement S does not rule out the possibility that something other than rain, such as melting snow, can make the sidewalks wet. Or suppose that in addition to statement S, we are told that it didn't rain. Can we legitimately conclude that the sidewalks did not get wet? Again no, and for the same reason: statement S does not rule out the possibility that something other than rain can make the sidewalks wet.

UNDERSTANDING THE IMPACT OF ADDITIONAL INFORMATION

The LSAT typically includes several questions that test your ability to see how additional facts bear on an argument. These questions may focus on facts that strengthen an argument, they may focus on facts that weaken the argument, or they may merely ask what additional information, if it were available, would be useful in evaluating the strength of the argument. Typical wordings of such questions are:

Which one of the following, if true, most strengthens the argument?

Which one of the following, if true, most weakens the argument?

In order to evaluate the argument, which one of the following would it be most useful to determine?

> **TIP.** When the qualifier "if true" appears in this kind of question, it tells you not to be concerned about the actual truth of the answer choices. Instead, you should consider each answer choice as though it were true. Also, consider each answer choice independently of the others, since it is not necessarily the case that the answer choices can all be true together.

Questions of this kind are based on arguments that—like most real-life arguments—have premises that provide some grounds for accepting the conclusion, but fall short of being decisive arguments in favor of the conclusion. For an argument like this, it is possible for additional evidence to make the argument stronger or weaker. For example, consider the following argument:

A survey of oil-refinery workers who work with MBTE, an ingredient currently used in some smog-reducing gasolines, found an alarming incidence of complaints about headaches, fatigue, and shortness of breath. Since gasoline containing MBTE will soon be widely used, we can expect an increased incidence of headaches, fatigue, and shortness of breath.[11]

The incidence of complaints about headaches, fatigue, and shortness of breath among oil-refinery employees who work with MBTE is, on the face of it, evidence for the conclusion that widespread use of gasoline containing MBTE will make headaches, fatigue, and shortness of breath more common. However, additional information could, depending on what this information is, make the argument stronger or weaker.

For example, suppose it is true that most oil-refinery workers who do not work with MBTE also have a very high incidence of headaches, fatigue, and shortness of breath. This would provide evidence that it is not MBTE but some other factor that is primarily responsible for these symptoms. But if we have evidence that something other than MBTE is causing these symptoms, then the argument provides only very weak support, if any, for its conclusion. That is, the argument's original premises, when combined with the additional information, make a much weaker case for the argument's conclusion than those premises did alone. In other words, the new information has made the argument weaker.

Of course, different additional evidence would make the argument stronger. For example, suppose that gasoline containing MBTE has already been introduced in a few metropolitan areas, and since it was first introduced, those areas have reported increased complaints about headaches, fatigue, and shortness of breath. This would provide evidence that when MBTE is used as a gasoline additive, it increases the incidence of these symptoms not just among refinery workers who work closely with it but also among the general public. So we now have evidence that is more directly relevant to the argument's conclusion. Thus, we now have a stronger case for the argument's conclusion; in other words, the new evidence has made the argument stronger.

We have seen that when new information makes an argument stronger, that information, together with the argument's original premises, makes a stronger case for the argument's conclusion than do the original premises alone. There are several ways in which this could work. The additional information could eliminate an obvious weak spot in the original argument. Alternatively, there may be no obvious weak spot in the original argument; the case for the argument may simply become even stronger with the addition of the new evidence. In some cases, the additional information will be something that helps establish the argument's conclusion, but only when combined with the argument's existing premises. In other cases, the new information will provide a different line of reasoning in addition to that provided by the original premises. The information that strengthens the argument about MBTE is an example of something that provides a different line of reasoning for the conclusion. In still other cases, the additional information will strengthen the argument by ruling out something that would have weakened the argument. And of course, additional information may weaken an argument in corresponding ways.

AN EXAMPLE
Consider this argument:

A recent study reveals that television advertising does not significantly affect children's preferences for breakfast cereals. The study compared two groups of children. One group had watched no television, and the other group had watched average amounts of television and its advertising. Both groups strongly preferred the sugary cereals heavily advertised on television.[12]

The conclusion of the argument is that television advertising does not significantly affect children's preferences for breakfast cereals. As evidence for this conclusion, the argument presents the results of a study comparing two groups of children: the study found that children in both groups—those who watched no television and those who watched average amounts of television and its advertising—strongly preferred the sugary cereals heavily advertised on television. On the face of it, the study results do seem to provide some support, although not conclusive support, for the argument's conclusion; if television advertising did significantly affect children's preferences, then we'd expect the children who watched television to have different preferences than the children who didn't watch television.

Here is the question:

Which one of the following statements, if true, most weakens the argument?

Let's consider an answer choice:

Most of the children in the group that had watched television were already familiar with the advertisements for these cereals.

Does this information weaken the argument? It suggests that even if the television advertising influenced the preferences of the children who watched television, this influence occurred some time ago. But this does not really imply anything about whether the advertising did influence the children's preferences. So the information provided by this answer choice neither strengthens nor weakens the argument.

Let's consider another answer choice:

Both groups rejected cereals low in sugar even when these cereals were heavily advertised on television.

This information may well be relevant to the argument's conclusion since it suggests that if a cereal is unappealing to children, then even a great deal of television advertising will not change the children's preferences. But this would provide additional evidence **in favor of** the argument's conclusion that television advertising does not significantly affect children's cereal preferences. So this answer choice strengthens the argument rather than weakens it.

[12]See Appendix B, page 86.

TIP. In questions that ask what weakens an argument, often one or more incorrect answer choices will provide evidence that strengthens the argument (or vice versa in the case of questions that ask for a strengthener). By the time you've read several answer choices, it is easy to forget what the question is asking for and pick an answer choice because it is clearly relevant—even though it's the opposite of what the question is asking for. It is important to keep the question clearly in mind in order to guard against making this kind of mistake.

Consider a third answer choice, then:

The preferences of children who do not watch television advertising are influenced by the preferences of children who watch the advertising.

How does this information affect the argument? Well, the reason originally offered for the conclusion is that the two groups of children do not differ in their preferences. But if the preferences of the children who do not watch television advertising are influenced by the preferences of those who do watch it, then the fact that the two groups do not differ in their preferences provides little, if any, reason to think that none of the children's preferences were affected by television advertising. After all, it could well be that the preferences of the children who watched television were strongly influenced by the advertising, and these children's preferences in turn strongly influenced the preferences of those who did not watch television, with the result being that the two groups had the same preferences. So when combined with the additional information, the argument's original premises make a much weaker case for the argument's conclusion than they did alone. Thus, this is the correct answer.

Some Points to Consider

- The additional pieces of information that weaken an argument generally do not challenge the truth of the argument's explicit premises. They are pieces of information that call into question whether the conclusion is strongly supported by those premises.

- Keep in mind that additional information may strengthen (or weaken) an argument only to a small extent, or it may do so to a large extent. When the question asks for a strengthener, an answer choice will be correct even if it strengthens the argument only slightly, provided that none of the other answer choices strengthen the argument significantly. On the other hand, if one answer choice strengthens the argument a great deal, then answer choices that strengthen only slightly are incorrect. For most questions that ask for weakeners, the correct answer will weaken the argument to some extent, but the premises will still provide some support for the conclusion. However, for some of these questions, the correct answer will eliminate all or almost all of the argument's original strength.

- Beware of answer choices that are relevant to the general subject matter, but not relevant to the way the argument supports its conclusion. A weakener or strengthener must affect the support for the conclusion. For example, consider the argument about gasoline containing MBTE. Suppose that adding MBTE to gasoline dramatically increased the price of gasoline. This information would be relevant if the argument's conclusion were broader, for example, if it concluded that gasoline containing MBTE should be widely used. Since the argument, however, is narrowly focused on whether widespread use of gasoline containing MBTE will increase the incidence of headaches, fatigue, and shortness of breath, the increased cost resulting from adding MBTE to gasoline is irrelevant and thus would neither strengthen nor weaken the argument.

- Similarly, for new information to weaken an argument, it must reduce the support that the premises provide for the conclusion. A fact may have negative connotations in the context of an argument but do nothing to weaken that argument. For example, consider the argument about television advertising and cereal preferences. Suppose that children who watch average amounts of television, unlike children who watch no television, do not get enough exercise. This would clearly be a negative aspect of watching television. But it doesn't weaken the support that the argument provides for the conclusion that television advertising does not significantly affect children's preferences for breakfast cereal.

ASSUMPTIONS

The Logical Reasoning section typically includes several questions that test your ability to identify assumptions of arguments. An assumption of an argument plays a role in establishing the conclusion. However, unlike a premise, an assumption is not something that the arguer explicitly asserts to be true; an assumption is instead just treated as true for the purposes of the argument.

Although assumptions can be stated explicitly in an argument, Logical Reasoning questions that ask about assumptions ask only about unstated assumptions. Unstated (or tacit) assumptions can figure only in arguments that are not entirely complete, that is, in arguments in which some of the things required to establish the conclusion are left unstated. There is thus at least one significant gap in such an argument.

Assumptions relate to the gaps in an argument in two different ways. An assumption is a **sufficient** one if adding it to the argument's premises would produce a conclusive argument, that is, an argument with no gaps in its support for the conclusion. An assumption is a **necessary** one if it is something that must be true in order for the argument to succeed. It is possible for an assumption to be both necessary and sufficient.

Sufficient Assumptions

Typical wordings of questions that ask you to identify sufficient assumptions are:

Which one of the following, if assumed, enables the conclusion of the argument to be properly drawn?

The conclusion follows logically from the premises if which one of the following is assumed?

AN EXAMPLE
Vague laws set vague limits on people's freedom, which makes it impossible for them to know for certain whether their actions are legal. Thus, under vague laws people cannot feel secure.[13]

The question you're asked about this argument is:

The conclusion follows logically if which one of the following is assumed?

In order to approach this question, you first have to identify the conclusion of the argument and the premises offered in its support. In this case, the conclusion is signaled by the conclusion indicator "thus" and reads "…under vague laws people cannot feel secure." Two considerations are explicitly presented in support of this conclusion. First, that vague laws set vague limits on people's freedom, and second, that having vague limits set on their freedom makes it impossible for people to know for certain whether their actions are legal. Note that the premises, though they tell us certain things about vague laws, make no explicit reference to whether people feel secure, and not feeling secure is what the conclusion

is about. For the conclusion to follow logically, this gap has to be bridged.

At this point, you are ready to look at the answer choices. Here are two of them:

(A) *People can feel secure only if they know for certain whether their actions are legal.*

(B) *If people know for certain whether their actions are legal, they can feel secure.*

Your task is to identify the answer choice that, together with the premises you've been given, will provide conclusive support for the conclusion.

So is (A) that answer choice? The explicit premises of the argument tell you that under vague laws people cannot know for certain whether their actions are legal. (A) tells you that if people do not know for certain whether their actions are legal, they cannot feel secure. So putting the explicit premises and (A) together, you can infer that under vague laws people cannot feel secure. And this is, in fact, the conclusion of the argument. So the conclusion follows logically if (A) is assumed.

Now, let's consider why assuming (B) is not sufficient to ensure that the argument's conclusion follows logically. (B) tells us about one circumstance in which people **can** feel secure. However, the argument's conclusion will not follow logically without the right kind of information about the circumstances in which people **cannot** feel secure. (B) does not give us any such information directly. Moreover, we cannot infer such information from what (B) does tell us. After all, it's perfectly compatible with (B) that people can feel secure in some circumstances in addition to the one (B) describes. For example, perhaps people can feel secure if they know for certain that they will not be prosecuted for their actions. Thus, since (B) tells us nothing about circumstances in which people cannot feel secure, it has nothing to contribute to reaching the argument's conclusion that people cannot feel secure under vague laws.

Some Points to Consider

• In answering sufficient assumption questions, you need to find a link between the stated premises and the conclusion. Try to determine from the explicit parts of the argument what logical work that link needs to do. Finally, look among the answer choices for one that can do that logical work and that, taken along with the explicit premises, allows the conclusion to be properly inferred.

[13]See Appendix B, page 86.

- In trying to figure out what logical work the link needs to do, don't get too specific. For example, what can be said about the logical work required of the link in the argument about vague laws analyzed above? It has to link something that has been explicitly connected with vague laws to an inability to feel secure. But there are two things like that: vague limits on people's freedom, and the impossibility of knowing for certain whether one's actions are legal. What this means is that answer choice (A) was not the only possible sufficient assumption here. An equally acceptable sufficient assumption would have been, "People cannot feel secure if they have vague limits on their freedom." So don't approach the answer choices with too specific a view of what you're looking for.

- When trying to identify a sufficient assumption, keep in mind that the correct answer must, when added to the argument's explicit premises, result in a conclusive argument; that is, in an argument that fully establishes its conclusion (provided that the explicit premises and the added assumption are all true).

Necessary Assumptions

Typical wordings of questions that ask you to identify necessary assumptions include the following:

The argument relies on assuming which one of the following?

The argument depends on the assumption that

Which one of the following is an assumption required by the argument?

Questions about necessary assumptions refer to arguments that, while not completely spelled out, do present a comprehensible case for accepting their conclusion on the strength of evidence explicitly presented. But if you look closely at the grounds offered for the conclusion and at the conclusion itself, you find that the evidence explicitly presented falls short of establishing the conclusion. That is, there is at least one significant gap in the argument.

EXAMPLE 1
Since Mayor Drabble always repays her political debts as soon as possible, she will almost certainly appoint Lee to be the new head of the arts commission. Lee has wanted that job for a long time, and Drabble owes Lee a lot for his support in the last election.[14]

As far as its explicit premises go, this argument leaves important matters unresolved. In order for the argument to show that Lee is the likely appointee, there can't be anyone else to whom Drabble has owed such a large and long-standing political debt and for whom this appointment would be adequate repayment. This idea of there being no one ahead of Lee in line is the sort of unstated but indispensable link in the support for the conclusion that we mean when we speak of a necessary assumption of an argument.

It can readily be shown that the assumption sketched above is in fact indispensable to the argument. Suppose the situation were otherwise and there were a person to whom Mayor Drabble owed a political debt that is of longer standing than her debt to Lee, and suppose further that the appointment could reasonably be viewed as paying off that debt. In this hypothetical circumstance, the fact that Mayor Drabble always repays her political debts as soon as possible would no longer point to Lee as the likely choice for the appointment. In fact, the argument above would fail. If the argument is to succeed, there cannot be another, better-positioned candidate for the appointment. And the argument depends on the assumption that there isn't any better-positioned candidate.

A Test for Necessary Assumptions

Necessary assumption questions, then, require you to identify tacit assumptions. The method for testing necessary assumptions that was introduced above in analyzing Mayor Drabble's situation is quite generally applicable, and for good reason. A necessary assumption is an indispensable link in the support for the conclusion of an argument. Therefore, an argument will be ineffective if a necessary assumption is deemed to be false. This points to a useful test: to see whether an answer choice is a necessary assumption, suppose that what is stated in that answer choice is **false**. If under those circumstances the premises of the argument fail to support the conclusion, the answer choice being evaluated is a necessary assumption.

EXAMPLE 2

The test for necessary assumptions can be used with the following argument:

Advertisement: Attention pond owners! Ninety-eight percent of mosquito larvae in a pond die within minutes after the pond has been treated with BTI. Yet BTI is not toxic to fish, birds, animals, plants, or beneficial insects. So by using BTI regularly to destroy their larvae, you can greatly reduce populations of pesky mosquitoes that hatch in your pond, and can do so without diminishing the populations of fish, frogs, or beneficial insects in and around the pond.[15]

The question asks:

Which one of the following is an assumption on which the argument depends?

Before you look for a necessary assumption, you need to get clear about the structure of the argument. The conclusion is that regular applications of BTI in a pond can, without reducing populations of assorted pond life, greatly reduce the numbers of mosquitoes that emerge from the pond. The evidence is that BTI kills almost all of the mosquito larvae in the pond, but does not kill (or even harm) other pond life.

The case that the argument makes for its conclusion is straightforward. Applications of BTI, by killing mosquito larvae, prevent the adult mosquito population from being replenished, but they have no direct effect on the other populations. So the argument concludes that, of the populations under consideration, only the mosquito populations will decline.

The first answer choice reads:

The most effective way to control the numbers of mosquitoes in a given area is to destroy the mosquito larvae in that area.

Now we apply the test for necessary assumptions by asking whether the argument would fail if this answer choice were false. That is, would it fail if the destruction of mosquito larvae were not the most effective way to control the numbers of mosquitoes? Definitely not. For one thing, the argument is not concerned with mosquito control alone, but speaks to a dual purpose, that of controlling mosquitoes while leaving other creatures unaffected. So the potential existence of any mosquito-control regimen, however effective, that did not spare other pond creatures would be beside the point. For another thing, the

argument merely concludes that the use of BTI works, not that it works better than all other methods. So the denial of this answer choice does not interfere with the support that the conclusion receives from the evidence presented. But if this answer choice were a necessary assumption, denying it would interfere with that support.

Now consider a second answer choice:

The fish, frogs, and beneficial insects in and around a pond-owner's pond do not depend on mosquito larvae as an important source of food.

Applying the test, we ask whether the argument would fail if this answer choice were false (that is, if these creatures did depend on mosquito larvae for food). Yes it would; after all, if the use of BTI means that fish, frogs, and so forth will be deprived of a food (mosquito larvae) that is important for them, then there is no reason to conclude that these creatures will survive in undiminished numbers. So denying the answer choice under consideration would cause the argument to fail; we have found a necessary assumption.

Some Points to Consider

• As you can see from the characterization of necessary assumptions given above, they are (unstated) constituents of arguments. Whether or not the author of the argument had a particular assumption in mind is not relevant to the issue. It is important to remember that identifying necessary assumptions is a matter of logically analyzing the structure of an argument, not a matter of guessing the beliefs of the arguer.

• For the purpose of *identifying* a necessary assumption, it is not necessary or even useful to evaluate whether that assumption is actually true, or how likely it is to be true. Identifying an assumption is a matter of probing the structure of an argument and recognizing hidden parts of that structure.

• An argument may have more than one necessary assumption. For example, the argument in Example 2 ignores the fact that a small proportion of mosquito larvae in a pond are not killed by BTI. But if there is a genetic basis for their not being killed, one might imagine that regular applications of BTI in a given pond will make it more and more likely that the mosquitoes left to breed with one another will be BTI-resistant ones that will likely produce BTI-resistant offspring. This population of BTI-resistant mosquitoes might then grow, without being kept in check by further applications of BTI, contrary to the drift of the argument. So the argument also depends on assuming that the two percent of mosquito larvae not killed by an initial application of BTI do not constitute an initial breeding pool for a BTI-resistant population of mosquitoes.

An argument can thus have more than one necessary assumption. Of course, only one of them will appear among the answer choices. But the one that does appear may not be one that occurred to you when you analyzed the argument. So it is a good idea not to prejudge what the correct answer will be. Instead, keep an open mind and examine each of the answer choices in turn.

- As indicated above, an argument may have more than one gap. Any one necessary assumption will address only one such gap. Moreover, a necessary assumption will often address only some aspects of a gap. In Example 2, the gap addressed by the necessary assumption—The fish, frogs, and beneficial insects in and around a pond-owner's pond do not depend on mosquito larvae as an important source of food—is, broadly speaking, that BTI does not kill the fish, frogs, and beneficial insects indirectly. But food deprivation is not the only way that BTI might kill those creatures indirectly. For example, as the mosquito larvae killed by applications of BTI decay, they might harm fish, frogs, and beneficial insects.

So do not reject an answer choice as a necessary assumption merely on the grounds that the argument, even if you make that necessary assumption, is still not a strong argument.

PRINCIPLES

Some Logical Reasoning questions test your ability to apply general rules and principles and to understand their use. These questions can involve the use of principles in arguments, or they can involve applying principles to actions or states of affairs.

Principles are broad guidelines concerning what kinds of actions, judgments, policies, and so on are appropriate. Most principles spell out the range of situations to which they apply. Within that range of situations, principles often serve to justify the transition from claims about what is the case to conclusions regarding what should be done.

There are several kinds of questions involving principles. You may be given a principle and be asked which action conforms to it, or which judgment it justifies, or which argument relies on it. Alternatively, the question may present a judgment, decision, or argument and ask which

principle is appealed to in making that judgment, decision, or argument. Logical Reasoning questions may also involve principles in various other ways. For example, a question could ask which action violates a principle. You may also see Logical Reasoning questions that ask you to recognize two situations as involving the same underlying principle, where that principle is not stated.

Applying a Principle That Is Given

AN EXAMPLE
People who receive unsolicited advice from someone whose advantage would be served if that advice is taken should regard the proffered advice with skepticism unless there is good reason to think that their interests substantially coincide with those of the advice giver in the circumstance in question.[16]

The following question refers to this principle:

This principle, if accepted, would justify which one of the following judgments?

The correct answer is provided by the judgment that is presented below:

While shopping for a refrigerator, Ramón is approached by a salesperson who, on the basis of her personal experience, warns him against the least expensive model. However, the salesperson's commission increases with the price of the refrigerator sold, so Ramón should not reject the least expensive model on the salesperson's advice alone.

The task here is to check how well the particulars of the situation fit with the principle. Do the general terms in which the principle is expressed cover the specific circumstances of the situation?

So first you should ask, "Does someone in this situation receive unsolicited advice from someone whose advantage would be served if that advice is taken?" If the answer is "yes," then the case under consideration falls within the range of situations to which the principle applies. If the answer is "no," then the principle offers no guidance. In this situation, someone—Ramón—does receive advice. If Ramón took the advice, this would be to the advantage of the advice giver (the salesperson), because the salesperson would receive a higher commission than she would otherwise. Is the advice unsolicited? Yes, because the salesperson approached Ramón without his asking for help.

The next question you should ask is, "Does the situation culminate in a judgment that the advice should be regarded with skepticism?" The answer is again "yes." The judgment that Ramón should not reject the least expensive model solely on the salesperson's advice is a judgment that treats the advice given—to avoid buying the least expensive model—skeptically.

You are not quite done at this point. The principle restricts itself to situations in which the person giving the advice and the person receiving the advice do not have interests that coincide. So you need to ask one more question: "Is there reason to think that the interests of Ramón and those of the salesperson substantially coincide in this matter?" Since Ramón probably wants to spend no more than he has to and since the salesperson probably wants Ramón to spend freely, there is reason to think that in this matter their interests do not coincide. So the principle applies to the situation and justifies the judgment.

Identifying a Guiding Principle

In the example above, the passage contained a principle and you were asked which judgment it justified. There are also questions that present a judgment or argument in the passage and ask which principle justifies it.

AN EXAMPLE

Marianne is a professional chess player who hums audibly while playing her matches, thereby distracting her opponents. When ordered by chess officials to cease humming or else be disqualified from professional chess, Marianne protested the order. She argued that since she was unaware of her humming, her humming was involuntary and that therefore she should not be held responsible for it.[17]

The question that is based on this passage is:

Which one of the following principles, if valid, most helps to support Marianne's argument against the order?

To answer this question, you need to compare the specific circumstances presented in the passage with the principle presented in each answer choice. First, consider the following answer choice:

Of a player's actions, only those that are voluntary should be used as justification for disqualifying that player from professional chess.

Does this principle apply to Marianne's situation? Well, it is clear that the principle concerns which of a chess player's actions can appropriately be used as justification for disqualifying that player from professional chess. Since the argument in the passage is concerned with whether one of Marianne's actions—humming while playing—should disqualify her from professional chess, it definitely falls under the range of situations to which the principle applies.

The principle will help support Marianne's argument if it leads to a judgment that Marianne's humming while playing should not be used as justification for disqualifying her from playing. According to a subsidiary conclusion of Marianne's argument, her humming is involuntary (this is supported by the claim that she was unaware of it). The principle asserts that only voluntary actions should be used as justification for disqualifying a player from professional chess, so this principle, together with the subsidiary conclusion of Marianne's argument, leads to the judgment that Marianne's humming should not be used as justification for disqualifying her. Thus the principle does help support Marianne's argument.

For the sake of comparison, consider one of the other answer choices:

Chess players should be disqualified from professional chess matches if they regularly attempt to distract their opponents.

Does this principle apply to Marianne's situation? Yes, it apparently does since it is also about the conditions under which chess players should be disqualified from professional chess matches. So now you need to ask, does the principle establish, or help establish, the conclusion that Marianne should not be disqualified for humming during matches? The answer is no. This principle just gives one condition under which a chess player should be disqualified—when that player regularly attempts to distract opponents. Since Marianne's humming is, she argues, involuntary, we can conclude that she is not trying to distract her opponents. Thus the principle does not lead to the judgment that Marianne should be disqualified for humming. But this does not mean that the principle leads to the judgment that Marianne should not be disqualified. After all, it is compatible with the principle that there are other conditions under which a player should be disqualified, and such conditions could include humming while playing. So the principle does not lead to the conclusion that Marianne should not be disqualified from professional matches and thus does not provide any support for Marianne's argument.

CROSS-REFERENCE. Making a common reasoning error known as confusion between "sufficient conditions" and "necessary conditions" could lead one to pick this answer choice. There are many opportunities for this confusion to arise in principles questions. Further discussion of this topic, and of correct and incorrect ways of reasoning with conditions, can be found on pages 29–31 under "Necessary Conditions and Sufficient Conditions."

Note that the process of finding the correct answer to a question that asks you to identify a guiding principle is basically the same as it is for a question that asks you to apply a given principle. The task is to make sure that a principle, which will be couched in general terms, fits the particulars of the situation. The only difference is that in the one case you need to check five different situations against one principle, and in the other case you need to check a single situation against five different principles. But the way you determine the best fit is the same. You check the principle for applicability, and you check to see whether the judgment, decision, recommendation, or action is in line with what the principle says.

Some Points to Consider

- Although principles always go beyond the particular case, they can vary enormously in degree of generality and abstractness. For example, the principle in the question about Ramón's refrigerator shopping is very general, applying to anyone who receives unsolicited advice. In contrast, the principle in the question about Marianne the chess player is more specific, applying only to professional chess players. And some questions have principles that can be even more specific than this. So be sure not to reject a principle as a correct answer solely because it seems to be too specific.

- When answering questions involving principles, it is always a good idea to check all of the answer choices. There is no sure way to determine whether a given answer choice provides the best fit except by considering and comparing all of the answer choices.

- Don't reject a principle as providing justification for an argument merely because it seems to do no more than spell out what the argument takes for granted. For example, someone might say, "Gerry sees very poorly without glasses. Therefore, Gerry should always wear glasses when driving." A principle justifying this judgment might be "Anyone who needs glasses to see well should always wear glasses when driving."

- Don't worry about the legitimacy of any of the principles you are presented with. Do not reject an answer because the principle involved is one that you personally would not accept.

FLAWS IN ARGUMENTS

Identifying Argument Flaws
The Logical Reasoning section includes a number of questions that ask you to identify a flaw of reasoning that has been committed in an argument. Questions of this kind are worded in a variety of ways. Here are some examples:

The reasoning in the argument is flawed because the argument

The argument commits which one of the following errors of reasoning?

The argument's reasoning is questionable because the argument fails to rule out the possibility that

The reasoning above is most vulnerable to criticism on the grounds that it

Test questions about flawed reasoning require you to recognize how an argument is defective in its reasoning. They will not require you to decide whether or not the argument is flawed. That judgment is already made and is expressed in the wording of the question. Your task is to recognize which one of the answer choices describes an error of reasoning that the argument makes.

When an argument is flawed, the argument exemplifies poor reasoning. This is reasoning in which the premises may appear to provide support for the conclusion but actually provide little or no real support. Poor reasoning of this sort can be detected by examining the argument itself, without considering any factual issues that aren't mentioned in the argument.

TIP.

Logical Reasoning questions in the LSAT test your skills in reasoning and analysis, not what you know about any particular subject matter. Whether a premise is factually accurate is not relevant. So don't pay attention to the factual accuracy of an argument's premises. Focus instead on logical connections between the premises that the argument sets out and the conclusion that it draws.

Since the flaws that you'll be looking for are not specific to the subject matter but relate to the argument's logical structure, the characterization of those flaws can be quite general. That is to say, the flawed reasoning in an argument might be described in terms that also apply to other arguments that commit the same error of reasoning. So once you detect where a particular argument has gone wrong, you may then have to figure out which of several quite general descriptions covers the case.

EXAMPLE 1

Consider the following brief exchange:

Physicist: The claim that low-temperature nuclear fusion can be achieved entirely by chemical means is based on chemical experiments in which the measurements and calculations are inaccurate.

Chemist: But your challenge is ineffectual, since you are simply jealous at the thought that chemists might have solved a problem that physicists have been unable to solve.[18]

Here is the question that is based on this exchange:

Which one of the following is the strongest criticism of the chemist's response to the physicist's challenge?

Before looking at the answer choices, briefly consider what appears to be wrong with the chemist's response. Notice that the chemist claims that the physicist's challenge is ineffectual but doesn't actually engage the substance of the physicist's challenge. Instead, the chemist accuses the physicist of professional jealousy and dismisses the physicist's challenge purely on that basis. But there is no reason to think that a challenge, even if it is fueled by jealousy, cannot be on target. So the chemist's response can rightly be criticized for "getting personal."

Now consider two of the answer choices. One of them reads:

It fails to establish that perfect accuracy of measurements and calculations is possible.

This statement is certainly true about the chemist's response. The chemist does not establish that perfect accuracy is possible. But this is not a good criticism of the chemist's response because it is entirely beside the point. Establishing that perfect accuracy is possible would have, if anything, damaged the chemist's position. So the chemist's response cannot be legitimately criticized for failing to establish this.

Another answer choice reads:

It is directed against the proponent of a claim rather than against the claim itself.

This criticism goes to the heart of what is wrong with the chemist's response. The chemist dismisses the physicist's challenge because of the physicist's alleged motives for making it and never actually discusses the merits of the challenge itself. It is directed against the person rather than against the position.

In this example, the chemist's response is clearly irrelevant to the substance of the physicist's claim. The argument that the chemist presents seems more like a rhetorical ploy than a serious argument. Many arguments are flawed in much less dramatic ways, however. They may contain only a small logical lapse that undermines the integrity of the argument, like the following two examples.

EXAMPLE 2

Morris High School has introduced a policy designed to improve the working conditions of its new teachers. As a result of this policy, only one-quarter of all part-time teachers now quit during their first year. However, a third of all full-time teachers now quit during their first year. Thus, more full-time than part-time teachers at Morris now quit during their first year.[19]

Notice that the argument uses proportions to indicate the degree to which first-year teachers are quitting. It says that **one-quarter** of part-time first-year teachers quit and that **one-third** of full-time first-year teachers quit. The conclusion of the argument is not expressed in terms of proportions, however, but in terms of a comparison between quantities: **more** full-timers than part-timers quit during their first year.

[18]See Appendix B, page 88.
[19]See Appendix B, page 88.

Your task is to accurately complete the following statement:

The argument's reasoning is questionable because the argument fails to rule out the possibility that

Note that we are looking for a possibility that needs to be ruled out in order for the conclusion to be well supported. So let's consider one of the answer choices:

before the new policy was instituted, more part-time than full-time teachers at Morris High School used to quit during their first year

How would the argument be affected by this information? It tells us something about the way things were before the new policy went into effect, but it doesn't shed much light on the effects of the new policy. And there is no way to infer anything about how many part-time and full-time teachers are quitting now, after the policy was instituted. So this information has no effect on the support for the conclusion, and there would be no reason for the argument to rule it out. Failing to rule it out, then, would not make the reasoning questionable.

Let's go on to consider another answer choice:

Morris High School employs more new part-time teachers than new full-time teachers

So how would the argument be affected if there were more new part-time teachers than new full-time teachers? If there were more new part-timers than full-timers, then one-quarter of the new part-timers could outnumber one-third of the new full-timers. So it could be true that more part-timers than full-timers quit during their first year. Since the argument concludes that more full-timers than part-timers quit in their first year, this possibility needs to be ruled out in order for the conclusion to be well supported. Thus, this choice is the correct answer.

EXAMPLE 3

If Blankenship Enterprises has to switch suppliers in the middle of a large production run, the company will not show a profit for the year. Therefore, if Blankenship Enterprises in fact turns out to show no profit for the year, it will also turn out to be true that the company had to switch suppliers during a large production run.[20]

The question asks:

The reasoning in the argument is most vulnerable to criticism on which one of the following grounds?

This question tells you that you should be looking for a problem with the argument. When you analyze the argument, you can identify the problem if you recognize that there may well be other reasons for not showing a profit besides having to switch suppliers in the middle of a large production run. This points to a major oversight in the argument. At this point, you are ready to review the answer choices.

One answer choice says:

The argument is a circular argument made up of an opening claim followed by a conclusion that merely paraphrases that claim.

This gives a general account of an argument flaw, but close inspection shows that the Blankenship argument does not have this flaw. That argument's conclusion says something quite different from what was said in the argument's premise. The conclusion says that if there is no profit, then there was a switch in suppliers. The premise is superficially similar, but it says that if there is a switch in suppliers, then there will be no profit. So this answer choice is not a legitimate criticism.

Another answer choice reads:

The argument fails to establish that a condition under which a phenomenon is said to occur is the only condition under which that phenomenon occurs.

This is the correct answer. The argument could only succeed if it showed that switching suppliers in the middle of a large production run is the only condition under which the company will show no profit for the year. But the argument fails to establish this point. Note that this answer choice points out what is wrong with this particular argument using general terms that could cover many different arguments.

> **CROSS-REFERENCE.** This is an example of a common reasoning error: confusion between "sufficient conditions" and "necessary conditions." A more detailed discussion of this topic, and of correct and incorrect ways of reasoning with conditions, can be found on pages 29–31 under "Necessary Conditions and Sufficient Conditions."

Some Points to Consider

- When you begin a flawed reasoning question, you should first try to get fairly clear about just where the argument goes wrong. If you have a reasonably clear sense of what is wrong with the reasoning, you can then look for the answer choice that describes the kind of error you have identified. Keep in mind that the descriptions offered may be very general—ones that could also apply to arguments very different in subject matter from the one you're considering.

- Keep in mind that for an answer to be the correct answer, it is not enough for it to describe some aspect of the argument correctly. The correct answer must describe a flaw in the reasoning of the particular argument under consideration.

- When dealing with a flawed argument that contains quantitative or statistical information, always check to see that the reference groups mentioned in the argument are appropriate and consistent. An argument may, for example, present information about the percentage of primary school teachers who have degrees in education and go on to draw a conclusion about the percentage of people who receive degrees in education and go on to teach primary school. Detecting this shift in reference groups is the key to identifying the flaw in this argument. It is not unusual for argument flaws to involve subtle shifts such as this.

- Some flawed arguments involve errors in reasoning about the relationship between proportions and quantities. Example 2 is a case in point. That argument involves a shift from talk about proportions in the premises to a statement about relative quantities in the conclusion. In other arguments, there might be an illicit shift from quantities in the premises to proportions in the conclusion. So pay close attention to any shifts like these.

Matching Argument Flaws

In your test you will sometimes encounter logical reasoning questions like the following:

Which one of the following arguments is most similar in its flawed reasoning to the argument above?

It is best to approach these questions in a straightforward way. First, try to determine how the reasoning in the reference argument is flawed. Then go over the arguments in the answer choices until you find the one whose reasoning is flawed in just the same way.

The wording of the question tells you that the reference argument is in fact flawed in its reasoning and that at least one other argument is, too. There is no need to worry about the precise wording of that flaw: the question does not hinge on it. But you do need to get a reasonably clear idea of the kind of reasoning error committed, because you will be making a judgment about whether one of the answer choices matches that error.

For this type of question, incorrect answer choices can be of two kinds. Some present arguments that are perfectly good, so they don't contain any flaw at all, let alone one that matches the one in the reference argument. Others do present flawed arguments, but the reasoning errors in those arguments are clearly different from the one in the reference argument.

AN EXAMPLE
Consider the following argument:

If the majority of the residents of the apartment complex complain that their apartments are infested with ants, then the management of the complex will have to engage the services of an exterminator. But the majority of the residents of the complex indicate that their apartments are virtually free of ants. Therefore, the management of the complex will not have to engage the services of an exterminator.[21]

The question you are asked about this argument is

Which one of the following arguments contains a flawed pattern of reasoning parallel to that contained in the argument above?

This question directs us to look for a flawed **pattern** of reasoning in the reference argument and to look for an answer choice that contains a similarly flawed pattern. This means that we should look for an argument that takes the same flawed approach to establishing its conclusion as the reference argument does, even though the two arguments might not share other characteristics, such as subject matter.

So what exactly is the flaw in the reference argument? One of the argument's premises says that under a certain condition the exterminator will have to come, and the second premise says that this condition is not met. The argument concludes that an exterminator will not have to be hired. But it is not difficult to see that something is wrong with this way of arguing: the problem is that there may be other conditions under which an exterminator has to be hired. To use a concrete example, it may also be

 [21]See Appendix B, page 89.

true that if there is a rodent infestation in the apartment complex, the management has to call in an exterminator. So the fact that the condition about ants is not met is not a good enough reason for concluding that an exterminator will not have to be hired. Without offering any reasons for doing so, the argument treats one circumstance that would produce a certain result as though it were the only circumstance under which this result would come about.

The next step is to check the answer choices and find the one that exhibits the same flawed pattern of reasoning. So let's consider the following choice:

The number of flights operated by the airlines cannot be reduced unless the airlines can collect higher airfares. But people will not pay higher airfares, so it is not the case that the number of flights will be reduced.

Is this an instance of the same flawed pattern? This argument is like the reference argument in that one of its premises asserts that under a certain condition (airlines cannot collect higher airfares) something will happen (schedules will not be cut). But this argument is unlike the reference argument in that its second premise actually meets the condition set out in the first premise. We are told that "people will not pay higher airfares," so it stands to reason that airlines cannot collect higher airfares. And thus the conclusion—that the number of flights will not be reduced—follows from these premises. So this argument does not exhibit the same pattern of flawed reasoning as the reference argument. In fact, it does not exhibit flawed reasoning at all.

Let's try another one of the answer choices:

Most employees will attend the company picnic if the entertainment committee is successful in getting a certain band to play at the picnic. But that band will be out of the country on the day of the picnic, so it is not true that most employees will attend.

Is this an instance of the pattern you are trying to match? Again, there is a conditional statement: if a certain band plays at the picnic, most employees will attend. So again, under a certain condition, something will happen. In this argument, the second premise indicates that the condition will not be met. The band, being out of the country, will certainly not play at the picnic. The argument goes on to conclude that most employees won't attend the picnic. So, as in the reference argument, this conclusion says that the thing that would happen under the original condition will not happen.

This is an exact match of the pattern of reasoning in the reference argument, hence it is an exact match of the flaw. As with the reference argument, the flaw can be illustrated concretely. Suppose, for example, that if the entertainment committee hires a certain well-known comedian to perform at the picnic, most employees will attend. This shows that the conclusion could be false even if what the argument tells us about the band is true.

Some Points to Consider

- For this type of question, there is no need to decide whether the reference argument is flawed. You are told that there is a flawed pattern of reasoning underlying the argument. It is sometimes useful, however, to determine whether or not an argument in an answer choice is flawed. If such an argument is **not** flawed, it cannot be the correct answer, because it will not be a relevant match for the reference argument.

- Remember that, although you need to get a reasonably clear fix on the kind of reasoning error committed in the reference argument, you do not need to come up with a precise formulation of that error. Since you are not asked to put your understanding of the reasoning error into words, all you need is a solid intuitive grasp of where the reasoning goes wrong.

- With this type of question, you look for the argument that most closely matches the reference argument in terms of its flawed reasoning. So other similarities with the reference argument, such as in the way the argument is expressed or in its subject matter, are irrelevant. Two arguments can be expressed in very different ways, or be about very different things, even though they exhibit the same pattern of reasoning.

CROSS-REFERENCE. For a more extensive discussion of this point, see "Identifying the Parts of an Argument" on pages 20–21.

EXPLANATIONS

Some of the questions in the Logical Reasoning section require you to identify a potential explanation for some state of affairs that is described to you. Broadly speaking, these questions come in two types: one in which you need to find an explanation for one particular situation, and another in which you need to explain how two seemingly conflicting elements of a given situation can both be true.

In the first sort of case, the phenomenon to be explained will merely be something that one would not ordinarily expect, the kind of thing that makes people say, "There must be an explanation for this." Imagine, for example, that it is discovered that domestic cats with purely gray coats are, on average, significantly heavier than those with multicolored coats. A fact like this calls for an explanation. The wording of a corresponding question would be along the lines of:

Which one of the following, if true, most helps to explain the difference in average weights?

In the second sort of case, the phenomenon to be explained is more complex. You are not simply presented with one fact that seems to require an explanation. Rather, you are presented with statements that appear to conflict with one another, and your task is to identify the answer choice that most helps to resolve this apparent discrepancy. That is, you are to select an answer choice that explains not just one or the other of the apparently conflicting elements but explains how they can both be true. With this sort of question, the passage might say, for example, that people spend much less time reading today than they did 50 years ago, and yet many more books are sold per year now than were sold 50 years ago. A typical wording for this sort of question is:

Which one of the following, if true, most helps to resolve the apparent discrepancy in the information given above?

EXAMPLE 1
The situation that follows seems to call for an explanation. In this case, a software production company's decision to refrain from prosecuting people who illegally copy its program raises questions regarding the company's reasons.

The company that produces XYZ, a computer spreadsheet program, estimates that millions of illegally reproduced copies of XYZ are being used. If legally purchased, this number of copies would have generated millions of dollars in sales for the company, yet despite a company-wide effort to boost sales, the company has not taken available legal measures to prosecute those who have copied the program illegally.[22]

The question that is based on this situation reads as follows:

Which one of the following, if true, most helps to explain why the company has not taken available legal measures?

Incorrect answer choices such as

XYZ is very difficult to copy illegally, because a sophisticated anticopying mechanism in the program must first be disabled.

do nothing to help us understand the company's decision. They may, however, be relevant to some aspect of the situation. The answer choice above, for example, does suggest that those who do the illegal copying are knowledgeable about computers and computer software, but it doesn't throw any light on the company's decision not to prosecute.

The correct answer,

Many people who purchase a software program like XYZ are willing to purchase that program only after they have already used it.

on the other hand, does suggest a reason for the company to tolerate the use of illegal copies of its program: those copies happen to serve as effective marketing aids in many cases and lead to legal sales of the program. The company may think that it has more to lose than to gain from going to court in order to stop the illegal copying. At the very least, the correct answer tells us that there is a disadvantage for the company in stopping the illegal copying, and this helps to explain why no legal measures are being taken.

EXAMPLE 2
Of the five bill collectors at Apex Collection Agency, Mr. Young has the highest rate of unsuccessful collections. Yet Mr. Young is the best bill collector on the agency's staff.[23]

This situation has an air of paradox. It seems clear that a superior ability to bring a collection effort to a successful conclusion is what makes one bill collector better than another. So how can Mr. Young, who has the lowest rate of successful collections, be the best bill collector? This is the focus of the question that goes along with this situation:

Which one of the following, if true, most helps to resolve the apparent discrepancy?

[22]See Appendix B, page 89.
[23]See Appendix B, page 89.

Consider the following answer choice:

Mr. Young's rate of collections per year has remained fairly steady in the last few years.

This gives us information that is pertinent to Mr. Young's performance as a bill collector. But it gives us no reason to think that Mr. Young could be the best bill collector at the agency despite having the lowest collection rate. It only gives us more reason to think Mr. Young is a poor bill collector, because it allows us to infer that his collection rate has been low for years.

Now consider another choice:

Mr. Young is assigned the majority of the most difficult cases at the agency.

This gives us reason to think more highly of Mr. Young's ability as a bill collector, because it makes sense to assign the most difficult cases to Mr. Young if he is very good at collecting bills. And if his rate of success is relatively low, this is not really a surprise, because his cases tend to be more difficult. So this answer makes it clear how two facts that seem to be difficult to reconcile with one another can in fact both be true. This resolves the apparent discrepancy in a satisfying way.

Some Points to Consider

- The correct answers to these questions do not generally offer complete and detailed explanations. Rather, they present crucial information that plays an important part within an adequate explanation.

- Pay close attention to what you are asked to explain. In the case of simple explanations of a particular factual matter, the wording of the question will direct you specifically to the fact to be explained. In the case of explanations that resolve an apparent conflict, however, it is generally up to you to develop a clear picture of that conflict.

- In most cases, there is more than one way to explain a set of facts or resolve an apparent conflict. So it is generally not a good idea to work out several explanatory stories in your head before examining the answer choices. Go to the answer choices instead and, for each choice, determine whether it helps to explain or resolve the situation.

- Note that these questions are qualified by the expression "if true." This indicates that you do not have to be concerned about the actual truth of the answer choices. Simply consider each answer choice as though it were true.

A GUIDE TO READING COMPREHENSION QUESTIONS

HOW TO APPROACH READING COMPREHENSION PASSAGES

The Reading Comprehension section is intended to assess your ability to read, with understanding and insight, passages comparable in terms of level of language and complexity to materials you are likely to encounter in the study of law. The passages are selected so that they can be adequately understood simply on the basis of what they say; you won't need any specialized prior knowledge to understand Reading Comprehension passages. Any technical terms that you need to understand to answer the questions are explained in the passages and all of the questions can be answered on the basis of information given in the passages.

Typically, a passage has a single main point. Sometimes the main point of a passage is to present a controversial position and either attack or defend it. Sometimes it is to examine and critique someone else's view. Sometimes it is to explain a puzzling phenomenon. Sometimes it is to give an accurate historical account of some important development. All passages will present a number of considerations that are relevant to the main point of the passage; the roles these considerations play are largely determined by the nature of that main point.

So how should you approach a Reading Comprehension passage? The single most important thing is to get clear about the main thrust of the passage: what is the passage mainly trying to get across to the reader? Occasionally, a passage will contain a particular sentence that explicitly states the main point. Even when there is such a statement, however, it does not necessarily come at the beginning of the passage; it could occur anywhere in the passage. More often, a passage will just present its position, critique, account, or explanation and rely on the reader to see where the passage is going. So what you should do as you work through a passage is read attentively, but at the same time you should be aware that it is not necessary to absorb and retain all of the descriptive detail that the author presents along the way. Try to remain focused on the main business of the passage, because the entire passage is organized around that. Without a clear sense of what the passage is about, you are likely to make mistakes about the relative significance of the various subsidiary points that the passage raises in support of its central point.

Be Aware of Paragraphs and Transition Words

Shifts in focus and perspective occur frequently in Reading Comprehension passages. A passage might shift from one concern to another, from the particular to the general, from a positive view of a topic to a negative one, or from one person to another. To get a solid grasp of how a given passage works, you must be aware of what the different ideas presented in the passage are and, more importantly, how the ideas relate to one another. A reader therefore needs to track the ideas presented by the author and the nature of the transition from one to another in order to grasp the significance, within the passage as a whole, of what is being said at any given point in the passage.

One feature of passages that can be extremely helpful in determining exactly how they work is their division into paragraphs. Paragraphs tend to have a relatively narrow focus and often play well-defined roles within the passage as a whole. So, for example, when an author switches from citing support for a position to defending the position against a challenge, the switch is typically marked by starting a new paragraph. Consequently, by asking yourself what each paragraph does, you can put together a fairly accurate picture of the structure of the passage as a whole.

Still, not all shifts in focus or perspective coincide with the transition from one paragraph to the next; one or more shifts might occur within a given paragraph, or conversely, two or more paragraphs might share the same basic focus. Another useful indicator of significant shifts in Reading Comprehension passages is the use of words or phrases such as "however," "nevertheless," "on the other hand," "by contrast," "and yet," and others. If you pay close attention to these sorts of signals, they will help orient you to what the significant parts of the passage are, and they will alert you to when a significant shift in focus or perspective is taking place. Incidentally, authors often provide helpful signals of continuity as well as shifts; continuity is frequently signaled by means of words or phrases like "for example," "by the same token," "furthermore," "in the same vein," "moreover," "similarly," and others.

One final caution about understanding the author's point of view: many times authors compare competing positions or theories and ultimately endorse one position or theory over its competitors. A common technique used by authors in this type of passage is to present the ideas they ultimately intend to reject in the best light possible, at least initially. One advantage of this approach is that criticisms are much more damaging if they work against an idea that has been presented in its strongest form; another advantage is that an author who takes pains to be as fair and evenhanded as possible to his or her opponents gains greatly in credibility. But what this means for you is that it can be quite difficult to follow such passages if you do not monitor the author's stance very carefully. When the author of a passage presents an opponent's point of view in the best light possible, it can appear to the unwary reader that the author endorses a position that he or she actually rejects. All of the techniques discussed above so far in this section can help you keep oriented to where the author actually stands in passages like these.

Should You Read the Questions First?

Some of you may be wondering at this point about a commonly heard piece of advice—that you should read the questions first, and only then turn to the passage. You should, of course, feel free to try this strategy and use it if you find it helpful. It is our opinion, however, that most people will find this strategy to be unhelpful. There are several reasons for this.

First, all of the questions associated with LSAT passages fit into standard question types—questions that ask for the main point or main purpose of the passage, questions that ask what the author would agree or disagree with, questions that ask what can be inferred from the information in the passage, and so on. We will say more about these and other question types in the sections that follow; what matters here is that many of these questions, though based on very different passages, look similar from one Reading Comprehension set to the next. Through study and practice, you can familiarize yourself with the types of questions that are typically written for an LSAT passage. You will then be able to anticipate what many of the questions will look like without having to spend your valuable time reading them before you read the passage.

Of course, some of the questions that follow a given passage might not look exactly like others of the same type; some even appear to be unique. But even in these cases, you will probably still gain very little from reading the questions first: it takes work to remember questions as you read the passage, and your mental energy is probably better spent on simply trying to comprehend the passage. As we have discussed already, LSAT reading passages can be quite difficult, involving sophisticated ideas and complex relationships. Answering the questions correctly requires you to get a firm grasp of the big picture in the passage. If you read everything in the passage with an eye to answering questions about particular details rather than with full attention to the thrust of the passage as a whole, you can easily miss the main point of the passage, and you run the risk of failing to grasp what the author agrees and disagrees with as well. So though you might do well on the questions that ask about those details, you might very well increase your chances of getting other questions in the set wrong.

Finally, it is important to remember that in the actual testing situation you have to read four passages and answer about 27 questions in 35 minutes. Time is of the essence. You can read the questions before you read the passages, but you still have to read the questions again when you are ready to answer them (you won't remember precisely what every question asks). Assume for the sake of argument that it takes roughly five seconds to read each question without reading the responses. That adds up to more than two minutes just to read the questions in a single Reading Comprehension section. If you read them twice, you double that to more than four minutes.

HOW TO APPROACH READING COMPREHENSION QUESTIONS

After reading through the passage once, you should turn to the questions. At this point you will probably have a fairly good sense of what the passage as a whole is trying to say, how the passage is organized, and roughly where in the passage specific points are made or particular facts are mentioned. But even if you do not feel all that confident about your understanding of the passage, you should proceed to the questions anyway rather than rereading the whole passage. In most cases, the first question in a set will ask you about the main point or the main purpose of a passage. If you don't think you have a handle on the passage, you might be able to recognize the main point or purpose of the passage when you see it, and answering this first question will in turn help orient you to the passage as a whole and to the questions that follow.

Either way, you should not feel that you need to remember the passage in great detail in order to begin working on the questions. For example, a passage might talk about two theoretical accounts of the rationale for incarceration, rehabilitative and punitive, and provide detail—even important detail—about both. In reading this passage, you should try to develop a clear sense of the difference between the two accounts and a general sense of where each is discussed. But there would be no point in trying to commit all of the detail in the passage to memory. First, not everything—not even every important thing—in the passage is going to be asked about.

Second, if you have a general idea of how the passage is structured and where its key elements are located, it is easy to check on the relevant details by rereading just portions of the passage. In fact, even if you are fairly confident that you remember everything you need to answer a particular question, it usually is a good idea to confirm your answer by checking the relevant portions of the passage anyway. Only if you have absolutely no doubt about the answer to a question is it advisable to respond without consulting the passage at least briefly.

When you read the questions, you should carefully attend to how each question is worded. Many questions contain detail that is intended to direct you to the relevant information in the passage. For example, one passage discusses the conflict between philosophers who subscribe to a traditional, subjective approach to studying the mind and philosophers who support a new "objectivist" approach.[24] According to the passage, the "subjectivists" believe that the mind should be explored by means of investigating individual subjective experiences such as consciousness, pain, emotions, and the like; "objectivists" find this approach outdated, however, and they believe the study of the mind should be limited to "hard" data such as the transmission of nerve impulses in the brain. One question in this set asks:

According to the passage, subjectivists advance which one of the following claims to support their claim that objectivism is faulty?

The first thing this question tells you is that the correct response will be a claim attributed in the passage to the subjectivists. Other claims in the passage are attributed to the objectivists, and the author also makes a few claims of his or her own; obviously, none of these can be the correct answer. Moreover, the question tells you that the correct answer must be the claim made by the subjectivists as part of their argument that objectivism is faulty. At this point most test takers will recall that the views of subjectivists regarding the problems with objectivism are described in the first half of the passage, and more specifically, in the second paragraph. A quick glance at that portion of the passage will enable you to identify the correct response.

In this case, the views being asked about are not the author's view, but many questions do in fact focus on what the author says, believes, or might agree with. At the same time, as we noted above, authors of passages used in the LSAT often mention other people as making claims, presenting evidence, holding beliefs, or taking positions about whatever it is that the question is asking about. Again, it is important to pay very close attention to

whether a question focuses on the views or claims of the author, or those of another person or group discussed by the author.

There is one additional piece of advice that applies to all Reading Comprehension questions: in general, even if you are fairly sure you have found the correct answer, you should probably take at least a quick look at any answer choices that you have not already eliminated. Incorrect answer choices are often partially correct, and as a result incorrect choices can sometimes appear to be correct when you first read them. Sometimes, a consideration of the full set of answer choices will lead you to reject a wrong answer that you initially thought to be correct.

QUESTIONS ABOUT THE PASSAGE AS A WHOLE

As we said earlier, the first question in most Reading Comprehension sets will ask you to identify the statement that best expresses the central idea, main idea, or the main point that the passage as a whole is designed to convey. These questions come in three main varieties. A few will take the following form: "Which one of the following most accurately **summarizes** the contents of the passage?" As the question implies, you should try to identify the response that summarizes the passage most accurately.

The thing to remember about questions like this is that the correct response will be the one that covers the important material in the passage most completely. That is not to say that the correct answer is necessarily the longest one, but it does mean that the correct answer will be most inclusive of the major steps in the discussion in the passage. The thing to keep in mind is that for questions that ask for the best **summary** of the passage, the correct answer will be the most comprehensive and inclusive of the steps taken in the passage. This variant of main idea questions is fairly rare, however. We use them infrequently, and you may not encounter any when you take the test.

The second, and by far most common, variant asks you to identify the **main point**, **main idea**, or **central idea** of the passage. Rather than asking you to identify the answer that summarizes the passage the best, these questions ask you to identify the idea or point that is at the heart of the passage. The important thing to know about these questions is that they have a much narrower focus than summary questions do. To answer them correctly, you have to be able to identify the most important idea that the passage is trying to establish—the idea to which all other ideas in the passage are subordinated.

[24]See Appendix C, page 90.

The third variant offers five potential titles for the passage and asks you to identify the answer that would be the **best title**. This variant is related to the main point/main idea question inasmuch as the best title will be the one that touches most directly on the central idea or point of the passage. These questions are also relatively rare. If you come across one, focus on finding the title that contains the content you would expect to see in a standard statement of the main idea of the passage.

One important thing to know about main idea or main point questions is that an answer choice that captures something that is true about the passage is still not necessarily the correct answer. For one thing, that answer choice may also say something that is not true about the passage, in which case it cannot be, on the whole, taken as correctly expressing the main idea of the passage. On the other hand, an answer choice may even be accurate in its entirety in stating something said in the passage, but be about something that is only a side issue in the passage rather than the main idea of the passage.

It is also worth noting that that there is more than one way of expressing the main idea of a passage; as a result, you may not find an answer choice that expresses the main point the way you would have put it. But if you have a good grasp of the passage, the correct answer should come closer to the way you would put it than the other responses do. What this means, however, is that the advice we mentioned earlier—namely, that you should check all the answer choices before moving on to the next question—is especially important for main point questions. As you review all the answer choices, keep in mind that each of the incorrect answer choices will either say something about the passage that is simply false or will describe something that is in the passage and might even contribute to establishing the main point but is not itself that main point. And again, the correct answer will be the only answer choice that is both entirely accurate in its statement of what is in the passage and on target in terms of hitting on the most important idea in the passage.

In addition to questions about the main point, which deal with the content that the passage is intended to convey, there is another kind of question that deals with the function of the passage as a whole. This kind of question asks about the way the author proceeds in developing the main idea; that is, they are questions about how the passage is structured. Such questions ask how the passage proceeds, or how the passage is organized, or what the passage is primarily meant to convey, or what the primary purpose of the passage is. For example, a passage might present a puzzling phenomenon and offer an explanation for it. Or it might contrast two opposing views and develop a case for

preferring one to the other. Or it might summarize the history of a scientific dispute. The answer choices for questions of this sort won't track every twist and turn of the author's development of the main point but will instead be very broad characterizations of the way the main point is developed. So don't be concerned if the correct answer seems to contain very little detail. The incorrect answer choices will be at a similar level of generality but will clearly fail to capture how the passage as a whole is organized. An incorrect answer choice might describe something that goes on in a portion of the passage or it might not fit anything about the passage at all. In any event, though, it will not get at the main structural blueprint of the passage as a whole.

Note that questions about the structure or organization of the author's text are not always concerned with the passage as a whole. Occasionally there are questions that ask you about the organization of a single paragraph. To answer these, it is a good idea to reread the specific paragraph that the question asks about.

QUESTIONS ABOUT WHAT THE PASSAGE SAYS OR IMPLIES

For each Reading Comprehension passage, you will be asked questions about the various ideas conveyed by the passage. These questions can range from very basic and straightforward questions (what does the passage say, literally?) to more sophisticated questions (what does the author imply without saying it explicitly?) to quite complex and advanced questions (what can be inferred from evidence presented in the passage, independently of whether or not the author intended the implication?). We will discuss all of these types of questions, starting with those at the basic end of the spectrum.

Perhaps the most basic component of Reading Comprehension is simply that of grasping what the text says on a literal level, and some Reading Comprehension questions are designed to make sure that you have processed the passage accurately at this fundamental level. Questions that assess this skill might ask, "Which one of the following is stated in the passage?", "The author says which one of the following about X?", "The passage asserts which one of the following regarding X?", "According to the passage, what is true about X?", or something similar. Even though these questions are fairly straightforward, the correct answer will not be an exact word-for-word repetition of something stated in the passage. It will, however, typically consist of a very close paraphrase of some part of the passage. The idea is that you should be able to identify not the exact wording of something said in the passage, but rather the gist of it.

For example, one of the questions following a passage about muralism, a Mexican artistic movement,[25] reads:

Which one of the following does the author explicitly identify as a characteristic of Mexican mural art?

(A)   Its subject matter consisted primarily of current events.
(B)   It could be viewed outdoors only.
(C)   It used the same techniques as are used in easel painting.
(D)   It exhibited remarkable stylistic uniformity.
(E)   It was intended to be viewed from more than one angle.

In the passage the author asserts that the muralists' works "were designed to be viewable from many different vantage points." The correct answer is therefore (E), "It was intended to be viewed from more than one angle." Notice that the correct answer is a fairly close paraphrase of what the author had stated in the passage.

A similar example occurs after a passage that says at one point, "the lower regions of the Earth's mantle have roughly the same composition as meteorites."[26] The question reads:

According to the passage, the lower regions of the Earth's mantle are characterized by

(A)   a composition similar to that of meteorites
(B)   the absence of elements found in rocks on the Earth's crust
(C)   a greater stability than that of the upper regions
(D)   the presence of large amounts of carbon dioxide
(E)   a uniformly lower density than that of the upper regions

The correct answer is (A), "a composition similar to that of meteorites." Again, the phrase "similar to" is a straightforward equivalent of "roughly the same as." Recognition of what the author says is all that is required in this question; there is no need for any significant interpretation. Questions like this one might seem unexpectedly easy, especially to test takers for whom Reading Comprehension is a relative strength. Don't be put off by how easy such questions might seem, however, and in particular, don't assume that some sort of trick must be lurking in such easy-seeming questions. Just remember that some LSAT questions are designed to test fairly basic skills and are therefore necessarily easy.

Of course, the process of reading also typically depends on skills that are considerably more advanced than this

basic skill of comprehension of the literal content of a text, and other Reading Comprehension questions are designed to test these skills. Any complex piece of writing conveys much more to the attentive reader than what it explicitly states. Authors rely on this, and without having to think about it, readers typically process texts at the level of what they convey implicitly as well as at the level of what they say explicitly. In some cases, much of what a writer leaves out and relies on the reader to supply is subject-matter knowledge that the writer assumes the reader possesses. This is especially true when the writer and the intended readers are all thoroughly familiar with the same specialized subject matter: articles in professional journals are good examples of texts that rely on this sort of shared knowledge. It is important to note, however, that the **LSAT does not presuppose any specialized subject-matter knowledge**, so none of the questions in it test this kind of specialized reading.

There are, however, many other types of information that a writer leaves out and relies on the reader to supply: things whose inclusion in the reader's comprehension of a text is supported by what the text does explicitly state. Suppose, for example, that a writer states, "The closing of the factory caused additional damage to a regional economy already experiencing high unemployment." In saying this, the writer has not explicitly said that the closing of the factory occurred before the additional damage to the regional economy, but a reader who fails to understand that the closing preceded the damage has probably failed to understand the sentence as a whole. In fact, it is probably safe to say that a reader who lacks the ability to supply such inferences cannot be said to understand what he or she reads in general.

There are a variety of Reading Comprehension questions that assess this ability. For example, you might be asked what can be inferred from a passage or from some specific portion of the passage; what the passage suggests or indicates about some particular matter addressed explicitly in the passage; or what, according to the passage, is true of some particular matter.

Other questions might ask about what a passage conveys or implies about people's beliefs—for example, "It can most reasonably be inferred that the author would agree with which one of the following statements?" or "It can be inferred from the passage that the author most clearly holds which one of the following views?" or "It can be inferred from the passage that Ellison most clearly holds which one of the following views regarding an audience's relationship to works of art?" or "Given the information in the passage, the author is LEAST likely to believe which

[25]See Appendix C, page 91.
[26]See Appendix C, page 92.

one of the following?" In approaching such questions, you need to pay close attention to specifically whose beliefs the question asks about. The incorrect answer choices will often be beliefs held by people other than those the question is asking about.

What the correct answers to all such questions have in common—whether the questions ask about beliefs or about information—is that they are justified by something that is explicitly stated in the passage. Sometimes this may be no more than a single sentence; on the other hand, sometimes you may have to pull together information from various parts of the passage to identify the correct answer. In some cases, locating the part of the passage that justifies an inference is straightforward. In other cases, the relevant justifying information might not be where one would most naturally expect to find it. In still other cases, there is no single part of the passage that contains all the relevant justifying information.

Questions also vary widely in how closely the correct answers match the part of the passage that justifies them. Sometimes, the correct answer does not go much beyond a slight rephrasing of the explicit content of the passage. For example, one passage discusses Richard A. Posner's critique of the law-and-literature movement, a movement that advocates the use of "techniques of literary analysis for the purpose of interpreting laws and in the reciprocal use of legal analysis for interpreting literary texts."[27] One question for this passage asks:

The passage suggests that Posner regards legal practitioners as using an approach to interpreting law that

(A) *eschews discovery of multiple meanings*
(B) *employs techniques like deconstruction*
(C) *interprets laws in light of varying community standards*
(D) *is informed by the positions of literary critics*
(E) *de-emphasizes the social relevance of the legal tradition*

The correct answer is (A), "eschews discovery of multiple meanings." What the passage explicitly says is that Posner asserts that "legal interpretation is aimed at discovering a single meaning." The reasoning involved in answering this question is quite straightforward: the passage does not come right out and say that Posner believes that legal practitioners eschew discovery of multiple meanings, but on the other hand it does not take much work to see that "eschew[ing] the discovery of multiple meanings" is the flip side of "to aim at discovering a single meaning." If you can remember the relevant part of the passage or find it quickly, you will find this question and others like it to be quite easy.

Other questions involve identifying the implicit ideas underlying a particular assertion made in a passage. In such cases, the connection between what the passage says and what the correct answer says is often less direct than in the last example, though the connection may still be somewhat easy to see. For example, after a passage concerning harmful bacteria that attack crops,[28] one question reads:

It can be inferred from the passage that crop rotation can increase yields in part because

(A) *moving crop plants around makes them hardier and more resistant to disease*
(B) *the number of Pseudomonas fluorescens bacteria in the soil usually increases when crops are rotated*
(C) *the roots of many crop plants produce compounds that are antagonistic to phytopathogens harmful to other crop plants*
(D) *the presence of phytopathogenic bacteria is responsible for the majority of plant diseases*
(E) *phytopathogens typically attack some plant species but find other species to be unsuitable hosts*

The correct answer is (E), "phytopathogens typically attack some plant species but find other species to be unsuitable hosts." The support for this answer is found in the first paragraph, where the author states:

Cultivation of a single crop on a given tract of land leads eventually to decreased yields. One reason for this is that harmful bacterial phytopathogens, organisms parasitic on plant hosts, increase in the soil surrounding plant roots. The problem can be cured by crop rotation, denying the pathogens a suitable host for a period of time.

Note that the passage says that crop rotation denies pathogens a suitable host for a period of time, but it does not provide an explanation as to why that strategy would work. It is left to the reader to fill in the gap by inferring what the relevant explanation is—namely, because crop rotation involves planting different crops in succession, and because pathogens that attack particular plants typically find other plants to be unsuitable hosts. This idea is not actually stated in the passage; it is instead an implicit assumption. In other words, this is a case in which the reader has to supply missing information in order to fully understand what the author says.

Some of you may have found that you supplied the missing information so quickly and so automatically that it hardly seemed like you drew an inference at all; as a result, you might think it odd that the question asks what can be inferred from the passage. But do not be thrown off if filling the relevant gap required little conscious effort for you. First, what was automatic and effortless for you may in fact require conscious effort on the part of other test takers. Second, questions like this one are designed to test your skill at high-level reading, and part of what defines that skill is the ability to supply relevant presuppositions when the author relies on you to do so. In short, even if, in your subjective experience of this question, the inference was so automatic that it seemed that little or no actual reasoning was required, logically speaking, you still had to draw an inference. This is a genuine skill that this type of Reading Comprehension question is designed to test.

Of course, there are questions in which the connection between the correct answer and the part of the passage that supports it is not so close. The following question involves a relatively large inference to get from the passage to the correct answer. A second question associated with the passage on Posner and the law-and-literature movement reads:[29]

According to the passage, Posner argues that legal analysis is not generally useful in interpreting literature because

(A) *use of the law in literature is generally of a quite different nature than use of the law in legal practice*
(B) *law is rarely used to convey important ideas in literature*
(C) *lawyers do not have enough literary training to analyze literature competently*
(D) *legal interpretations of literature tend to focus on legal issues to the exclusion of other important elements*
(E) *legal interpretations are only relevant to contemporary literature*

The correct answer is (A), "use of the law in literature is generally of a quite different nature than use of the law in legal practice."

Here is the part of the passage that supports this answer:

Critiquing the movement's assumption that lawyers can offer special insights into literature that deals with legal matters, Posner points out that writers of literature use the law loosely to convey a particular idea, or as a metaphor for the workings of the society envisioned in

their fiction. Legal questions per se, about which a lawyer might instruct readers, are seldom at issue in literature.

According to Posner, therefore, lawyers can be expected to be helpful about specific technical legal questions, but detailed analysis of technical legal questions is rarely at issue when the law is invoked, as it typically is in literature, to convey an idea or serve as a metaphor. So for Posner, the law as it figures in legal practice is very different from the law as it figures in literature. The correct answer, then, is justified by the text of the passage but is by no means a simple restatement of anything that is actually said there. A certain amount of interpretation is required to arrive at this answer.

Similarly, the following is an example of the more typical case of questions that ask what can be inferred from, or what is suggested by, the passage. The question asks:

It can be inferred from the passage that the author's view of Watteau's works differs most significantly from that of most late-nineteenth-century Watteau admirers in which one of the following ways?[30]

The correct answer is:

In contrast to most late-nineteenth-century Watteau admirers, the author finds it misleading to see Watteau's work as accurately reflecting social reality.

There is no statement of precisely this point anywhere in the passage. There are two points in this answer, and they have to be established separately. The first of these points is that most late-nineteenth-century Watteau admirers saw Watteau's work as accurately reflecting social reality. The clearest statement of this position comes in the first paragraph, in which we are told that nineteenth-century writers accepted as genuine the image Watteau had presented of his age (the early eighteenth century). Underscoring this point, the first paragraph ends with the statement that by 1884, the bicentenary of Watteau's birth, it was standard practice for biographers to refer to him as "the personification of the witty and amiable eighteenth century."

The second point contained in the correct answer is that the author does not see Watteau's work as accurately reflecting social reality. Watteau's work is characterized as lyrical and charming, and the century that it portrays as witty and amiable. But the author tells us in the second paragraph that the eighteenth century's first decades, the period of Watteau's artistic activity, were "fairly calamitous

[29]See Appendix C, page 93.
[30]See Appendix C, page 95.

ones." The author goes on to say that the year of Watteau's first Paris successes was marked by military defeat and a disastrous famine. For this question, then, justifying the correct answer requires you to identify as relevant, and then put together, various pieces of information that in the passage are interspersed among other pieces of information that have no bearing on the specific question asked.

One final comment on the general category of question we have been discussing in this section. We have been making a distinction between recognizing a paraphrase of something said in the passage and answering questions that require some interpretation or inference. But it may have occurred to some of you that this line can get quite blurry, especially if the paraphrase looks quite different from the original, or the inference seems fairly obvious. For example, think back to the question about crop rotation we discussed earlier (page 51). This question asks what can be inferred from the passage, and the correct answer is indeed an inference inasmuch as it is not stated explicitly, but is rather left implicit in the relevant part of the passage. But on the other hand, the implication is not really very far from the surface of the passage; as a result, identifying it may seem unexpectedly easy to some people.

As this example shows, it can be risky to judge answer choices by whether they are easier (or harder) than you expect the correct answer to be. The important thing to remember is that, whatever form the relationship between the passage and the correct answer takes, the correct answer is always the only answer choice that is truly supported by the passage. The incorrect answer choices might appear to be right at first glance, but they will always be found on closer inspection to have something about them that is wrong. Perhaps they are not really supported by the passage, or perhaps they even contradict the passage. As with all Reading Comprehension questions, you should judge the answer choices in questions about what the passage says or implies only by whether or not they are supported by the passage.

QUESTIONS THAT REQUIRE USING CONTEXT TO REFINE MEANING (MEANING IN CONTEXT)

Another skill a good reader brings to a text is the ability to interpret words and phrases not just as a dictionary would define them, but in a more specific sense identifiable from the way in which the author is using them in the particular text. In a given text, words and phrases do not appear in isolation but are embedded in the context of a narrative, an argument, an explanation, and so on. What this wider

context does, among other things, is clarify ambiguous expressions, narrow the meaning of vague expressions, or supply a definition for idiosyncratic uses of an expression.

Accordingly, the Reading Comprehension section typically contains questions that test the reading skill of ascertaining the contextually appropriate meanings of words and phrases. In some cases, this task is not very involved. For example, in a passage concerned with offshore oil production,[31] the second paragraph ends by saying:

> researchers have discovered that because the swirl of its impeller separates gas out from the oil that normally accompanies it, significant reductions in head can occur as it [a centrifugal pump] operates.

One of the questions following this passage reads:

> Which one of the following phrases, if substituted for the word "head" in line 47, would LEAST change the meaning of the sentence?
>
> (A) the flow of the crude inside the pump
> (B) the volume of oil inside the pump
> (C) the volume of gas inside the pump
> (D) the speed of the impeller moving the crude
> (E) the pressure inside of the pump

The word "head" is used here in a specialized sense not accessible to the ordinary reader. But the attentive reader of the passage at issue would have noticed that the previous paragraph ended with this sentence:

This surge in gas content causes loss of "head," or pressure inside a pump, with the result that a pump can no longer impart enough energy to transport the crude mixture through the pipeline and to the shore.

In other words, the precise sense in which the word "head" is used in this passage in connection with the operation of pumps has been explicitly clarified. Accordingly, the answer to the question that deals with the meaning of the word "head" here is "the pressure inside of the pump," or (E).

There are cases where contextual clarification is not as clear cut. Take as an example the opening sentence of the passage about the French painter Watteau:[32]

[31]See Appendix C, page 96.
[32]See Appendix C, page 95.

Late-nineteenth-century books about the French artist Watteau (1684–1721) betray a curious blind spot: more than any single artist before or since, Watteau provided his age with an influential image of itself, and nineteenth-century writers accepted this image as genuine.

One of the questions about this passage reads as follows:

The phrase "curious blind spot" (lines 2–3) can best be interpreted as referring to which one of the following?

(A) *some biographers' persistent inability to appreciate what the author considers a particularly admirable quality*
(B) *certain writers' surprising lack of awareness of what the author considers an obvious discrepancy*
(C) *some writers' willful refusal to evaluate properly what the author considers a valuable source of information about the past*
(D) *an inexplicable tendency on the part of some writers to undervalue an artist whom the author considers extremely influential*
(E) *a marked bias in favor of a certain painter and a concomitant prejudice against contemporaries the author considers equally talented*

The correct answer turns out to be (B), "certain writers' surprising lack of awareness of what the author considers an obvious discrepancy." You can see that the sentence in which the phrase "curious blind spot" actually appears does not provide nearly enough information to establish the correctness of this answer. No obvious discrepancy is revealed in that sentence, and also no indication that anyone was unaware of this discrepancy. All that can be inferred from the opening sentence of the passage is that the blind spot has to do with nineteenth-century writers accepting as genuine the image Watteau had provided of his age. It is not until we find, at the end of the first paragraph, a nineteenth-century description of Watteau as "the personification of the witty and amiable eighteenth century" that we can tell that the image that Watteau has provided was overwhelmingly positive. In the second paragraph we are told that "The eighteenth century's first decades, the period of [Watteau's] artistic creativity, were fairly calamitous ones." So here the "obvious discrepancy" is finally revealed. Given its obviousness, the fact that late-nineteenth-century writers were evidently not aware of it can reasonably be seen as surprising, or "curious." Notice, however, that a phrase that is introduced in the first sentence of the passage cannot be given the fully specific sense intended for it by the author until the end of the second paragraph has been reached.

QUESTIONS ABOUT HOW THINGS THE AUTHOR SAYS FUNCTION IN CONTEXT

A skilled reader has to be able to cope with the fact that writers, even good writers, do not make explicit why they say certain things in certain places. The reader has to be able to extract the function that certain expressions, phrases, sentences, or even paragraphs have in the context of a larger piece of writing. Sometimes the writer does use conventional cues to guide the reader in how to take what is being said. Such cues, though conventional, can be quite subtle. A good reader picks up on those cues and uses them in interpreting the piece of text to which they are relevant.

An example of a textual connection not made explicit at all occurs in the following lengthy excerpt from a passage about women medical practitioners in the Middle Ages.[33] First, a little background to place the excerpt in context: it begins with the phrase, "This common practice," which refers back to a practice discussed earlier in the same paragraph. According to the author, the typical practice among historians studying the Middle Ages is to take the term "woman medical practitioner," whenever it appears in medieval records, to mean "midwife." The relevant excerpt, then, reads:

This common practice obscures the fact that, although women were not represented on all levels of medicine equally, they were represented in a variety of specialties throughout the broad medical community. A reliable study by Wickersheimer and Jacquart documents that, of 7,647 medical practitioners in France during the twelfth through fifteenth centuries, 121 were women; of these, only 44 were identified as midwives, while the rest practiced as physicians, surgeons, apothecaries, barbers, and other healers.

There is no explicit statement in this passage of why the author chooses to cite the study by Wickersheimer and Jacquart. The sentence about that study simply follows the one preceding it. The reader is not specifically told how to connect the information in that sentence with information presented either earlier or later. For a skilled reader, though, the connection is obvious: the study presents scholarly, documented support for a claim that is made in the preceding sentence, namely that women were represented in a variety of specialties throughout the broad medical community.

[33]See Appendix C, page 97.

So for a question that asks:

The author refers to the study by Wickersheimer and Jacquart in order to

(A) demonstrate that numerous medical specialties were recognized in Western Europe during the Middle Ages
(B) demonstrate that women are often underrepresented in studies of medieval medical practitioners
(C) prove that midwives were officially recognized as members of the medical community during the Middle Ages
(D) prove that midwives were only a part of a larger community of women medical practitioners during the Middle Ages
(E) prove that the existence of the midwives can be documented in Western Europe as early as the twelfth century

The correct answer is (D), prove that midwives were only a part of a larger community of women medical practitioners during the Middle Ages.

This is so even though the author has not said anything like "As proof of this, the study by Wickersheimer and Jacquart may be cited." It is probably safe to say that a reader who does not make this connection on his or her own did not comprehend this part of the passage. For such a reader, the author's reference to the study by Wickersheimer and Jacquart will probably appear to come out of nowhere.

Now consider an example of a question that requires you to understand the way an author uses subtle cues to indicate the function of a piece of text. The passage on which the question is based reads, in part:

Critics have long been puzzled by the inner contradictions of major characters in John Webster's tragedies . . . The ancient Greek philosopher Aristotle implied that such contradictions are virtually essential to the tragic personality, and yet critics keep coming back to this element of inconsistency as though it were an eccentric feature of Webster's own tragic vision.[34]

This question asks:

The author's allusion to Aristotle's view of tragedy in lines 11–13 serves which one of the following functions in the passage?

(A) It introduces a commonly held view of Webster's tragedies that the author plans to defend.
(B) It supports the author's suggestion that Webster's conception of tragedy is not idiosyncratic.
(C) It provides an example of an approach to Webster's tragedies that the author criticizes.
(D) It establishes the similarity between classical and modern approaches to tragedy.
(E) It supports the author's assertion that Elizabethan tragedy cannot be fully understood without the help of recent scholarship.

The correct answer is (B), "It supports the author's suggestion that Webster's conception of tragedy is not idiosyncratic." The author's allusion to Aristotle's view of tragedy introduces the idea that a vision of tragedy similar to Webster's can be traced back to the ancient Greeks. So Webster's view cannot be regarded as idiosyncratic unless the critics are essentially prepared to dismiss Aristotle's view as unimportant. But what the author does is let Aristotle's view stand as authoritative by using it to portray the critics as wrongheaded. What the author says is that the critics view the element of inconsistency in Webster's characters "as though it were" eccentric. By using the phrase "as though it were" the author suggests that the critics are wrong. The author further says that the critics "keep coming back" to this element, thereby signaling a certain impatience with the stubbornness with which the critics hold on to their mistaken view. And the author says "and yet," thereby signaling that the critics hold on to their mistaken view in the face of clear evidence to the contrary, provided by Aristotle.

To understand how this type of question works, note that the author provides a variety of cues to indicate to the reader that the allusion to Aristotle is introduced to support the position, endorsed by the author, that Webster's conception of tragedy is not idiosyncratic. The cues are recognizable, but they are relatively subtle. There is no explicit statement of the author's position or of how the allusion to Aristotle bears on it.

In approaching questions about what the author's purpose is in using a certain word, phrase, or sentence, remember that unless that word, phrase, or sentence left you puzzled, you probably already understood the author's purpose as you made your way through the passage. The process involved here is essential and often subtle, but good readers typically exercise this skill automatically and unconsciously. One conclusion to be drawn from this fact is that you should not look for far-fetched interpretations of what the author's purpose was. Most probably the purpose that you automatically supplied in the process of reading is the correct one. If you were not able to appreciate immediately what the purpose of using a particular word, phrase, or sentence was, reread the immediate context. In a well-written text, the author generally supplies all the cues you need to understand the purpose of any part of the text right around that text. An author is not likely to hide hints as to the purpose of a particular choice of word two or three paragraphs away. A close reading of the immediate context will usually reveal what the author's purpose was.

QUESTIONS THAT REQUIRE THE RECOGNITION OF ANALOGOUS PATTERNS OR FEATURES IN DIFFERENT FACTUAL SETTINGS

One way for a reader to demonstrate an understanding of a fact pattern that is presented in a text (or of the way someone has made a case for a position) is by recognizing another fact pattern (or argument) as structurally similar. Questions that test this ability are typically included in the Reading Comprehension section.

Questions of this kind will direct you to something specific in the text and ask you to find something similar to it among the answer choices. The relevant part of the passage can be characterized insightfully in general terms, and this characterization has to fit the correct answer as well. What sorts of general terms? Typically, things of the following sort:

• One thing is a cause of another.

• One thing is a subset of another.

• One thing is mistaken for another.

• Some type of behavior is irresponsible.

• Something falls short of a particular standard.

• An action has consequences that are the opposite of those intended.

These examples are given only to illustrate roughly the kind of similarity that you will typically be looking for. They are not meant to suggest that you should first try to restate what is going on in the passage in such terms. What is crucial is a clear understanding of the relevant part of the passage. You don't need an explicit formulation; in fact, attempting to come up with such an explicit formulation may be a waste of your time.

To see what is involved here, let us consider a very simple case first. The question asks:

Which one of the following is most closely analogous to the error the author believes historians make when they equate the term "woman medical practitioner" with "midwife"?

(A) equating pear with apple
(B) equating science with biology
(C) equating supervisor with subordinate
(D) equating member with nonmember
(E) equating instructor with trainee

As we saw earlier when we considered another question from this set (page 54–55), the author asserts that historians do in fact equate the term "woman medical practitioner," whenever they encounter it in medieval records, with "midwife."[35] But the wording of the question further alerts us to the fact that historians who equate the two terms are committing a particular kind of error. The author's account of this error is presented in the following words: "This common practice obscures the fact that, although women were not represented on all levels of medicine equally, they were represented in a variety of specialties throughout the broad medical community." The author elaborates on this by saying that in a study of medical practitioners that included 121 women, only 44 of those women were midwives, whereas the rest practiced as physicians, surgeons, apothecaries, barbers, and other healers. So the error, stated in general terms, lies in equating a category with one of its subcategories. What you are asked to do is select the answer choice that presents the same error.

The correct answer is (B), "equating science with biology." Someone who equates science with biology would be ignoring the fact that the category of science includes many subcategories in addition to biology. Such a person would commit an error analogous to the one that the author believes historians make.

Notice that not everything about (B) is precisely analogous to the historians' equating of woman medical practitioners with midwives. For example, the terms equated in (B) refer to academic subjects and not to people. On the other hand, the terms equated in (C) and (E) do refer to people, just as do those equated by the historians. So why does the similarity in terms of people being referred to not matter? Because it is not part of what makes the historians' practice an error that they happen to be talking about people.

When you focus on finding errors analogous to the historians' error, you find that none of answer choices (A), (C), (D), and (E) make such an error. They all do make an error, and it happens to be the same kind of error in each case. They all equate terms, neither of which includes the other, whereas the historians equate terms, one of which—but only one of which—includes the other. What the historians get wrong is that they fail to see that not all woman medical practitioners were midwives, even though all midwives were medical practitioners. By contrast, what (A), for example, gets wrong in equating pears with apples is that it lumps together two categories, neither of which includes the other even partially.

Now let's look at a more complex example. In a passage concerned with certain interactions between the United States Bureau of Indian Affairs and the Oneida tribe of Wisconsin,[36] we are told that the Oneida were offered a one-time lump-sum payment of $60,000 in lieu of the $0.52 annuity guaranteed in perpetuity to each member of the tribe under the Canandaigua Treaty. We are then further informed that

> *The offer of a lump-sum payment was unanimously opposed by the Oneida delegates, who saw that changing the terms of a treaty might jeopardize the many pending land claims based upon the treaty.*

> *There is a question that is based on this rejection of the lump-sum offer and which reads as follows:*

> *Which one of the following situations most closely parallels that of the Oneida delegates in refusing to accept a lump-sum payment of $60,000?*

(A) *A university offers a student a four-year scholarship with the stipulation that the student not accept any outside employment; the student refuses the offer and attends a different school because the amount of the scholarship would not have covered living expenses.*

(B) *A company seeking to reduce its payroll obligations offers an employee a large bonus if he will accept early retirement; the employee refuses because he does not want to compromise an outstanding worker's compensation suit.*

(C) *Parents of a teenager offer to pay her at the end of the month for performing weekly chores rather than paying her on a weekly basis; the teenager refuses because she has a number of financial obligations that she must meet early in the month.*

(D) *A car dealer offers a customer a $500 cash payment for buying a new car: the customer refuses because she does not want to pay taxes on the amount, and requests instead that her monthly payments be reduced by a proportionate amount.*

(E) *A landlord offers a tenant several months rent-free in exchange for the tenant's agreeing not to demand that her apartment be painted every two years, as is required by the lease; the tenant refuses because she would have to spend her own time painting the apartment.*

What precisely is the situation of the Oneida delegates in refusing the lump-sum payment? It is an action (refusing the offer) that is motivated by a specific reason (concern that not taking that action might have undesirable legal ramifications). This is a rather broad characterization of the situation in which the Oneida delegates find themselves, but it turns out to be a description that applies equally well to the correct answer, and **only** to the correct answer. The correct answer is (B), "A company seeking to reduce its payroll obligations offers an employee a large bonus if he will accept early retirement; the employee refuses because he does not want to compromise an outstanding worker's compensation suit." What is parallel is the reason why an otherwise generous-seeming offer is refused.

Notice that there are some clear differences between the situation of the Oneida delegates and that of the employee. For example, in one case it is delegates refusing on behalf of a large group that would be affected by that decision, and in the other case a single individual refuses on his own behalf alone. But this difference plays no role in selecting the correct answer, even though it might be seen as a significant difference between the two situations. First, the fact that this important decision affecting the Oneida people as a whole was made by Oneida delegates, although mentioned in the passage, is not given any prominence anywhere in the passage. What the passage does focus on, in discussing the refusal of the lump-sum offer, is the reasons the delegates had for their refusal. So as the passage presents the situation, the reasons for the refusal are the central feature of the situation, and for another situation to be parallel, it would have to be parallel in this respect. Only the correct answer meets this requirement. Moreover, notice that all of the answer choices are like the correct answer in focusing on an individual, which means that it is not the case that any of the incorrect answers are more parallel to the passage even in this regard.

In fact, any scenario that is analogous or parallel to another one **has to be different** in some ways. Otherwise it would be identical to the first scenario, and not just analogous to it. So it is important to keep in mind that the correct answer to this type of question will be the one that is **most closely parallel** or **most analogous** or **most similar** to something discussed in the passage, even though it will necessarily be dissimilar in many respects.

QUESTIONS ABOUT THE AUTHOR'S ATTITUDE

Authors write things for a variety of reasons. They may just write to report, simply putting down what they take to be the facts, giving no indication of their own feelings, either positive or negative, about those facts. Or they may set down what someone else has reported as fact, without giving any indication of how that person feels about them or how they themselves feel about them. But often authors write with other purposes in mind. For example, they may write to persuade the reader of the merits of some position, in which case they typically write in such a way that the reader can tell that they have positive feelings with respect to that position. By contrast, they may write to warn the reader that a view has no merit, in which case they often make evaluative comments that allow the reader to infer what their attitude toward the matter is. Thus, one feature of a text that careful readers pay attention to is whether the author, by taking a certain tone, or by certain word choices, betrays any attitude other than bland neutrality toward the material he or she is presenting. Also of interest is whether any of the people mentioned by the author in the passage are presented as having any particular attitude toward anything that figures in the passage. These things are potentially important in evaluating what has been read. For example, if an author's attitude is one of boundless enthusiasm, a careful reader might take what that author says with a grain of salt.

In the Reading Comprehension section, you will encounter questions that ask directly about what the author's attitude is, or the attitude of people that the author discusses. Another kind of question may ask you to consider words or phrases that appear in the passage and to identify those that indicate the attitude of the author, or of people mentioned in the passage, toward some specific thing that is discussed in the passage.

When you are dealing with a question that asks directly about attitude, you should assess the passage with an eye to whether it contains indicators of tone or evaluative terms. For example, sometimes an initially positive tone is tempered later by an expression of reservations; or an initially rather dismissive tone might be moderated later

by a grudging admission of something worthwhile. The description of the author's attitude overall will reflect this and you should choose among the answer choices accordingly. An example will illustrate this point. The question reads:

The attitude of the author of the passage toward Breen and Innes's study can best be described as one of

(A) *condescending dismissal*
(B) *wholehearted acceptance*
(C) *contentious challenge*
(D) *qualified approval*
(E) *sincere puzzlement*

The correct answer is (D), "qualified approval." The first reference to Breen and Innes occurs early in the passage, in the sentence

In *Myne Owne Ground, T.H. Breen and Stephen Innes contribute significantly to a recent, welcome shift from a white-centered to a black-centered inquiry into the role of African Americans in the American colonial period.*[37]

The word "welcome" indicates approval, and since Breen and Innes are said to have significantly contributed to something that is welcome, the approval extends to them and their study. But this is not the only sign of the author's attitude. Much later in the passage, the author says that Breen and Innes "underemphasize much evidence that customary law, only gradually embodied in statutory law, was closing in on free African Americans well before the 1670's . . ." The verb "underemphasize" expresses a criticism of Breen and Innes' work, and so the approval indicated by "welcome" can no longer be regarded as unqualified. The correct answer, "qualified approval," does justice to both expressions of the author's attitude.

Sometimes you may be asked to identify the words or phrases in a passage that are indicative of the author's attitude toward something. A question of this sort might ask,

The author's attitude toward the "thesis" mentioned in line 56 is revealed in which one of the following pairs of words?

(A) *"biases" (line 5) and "rhetorical" (line 6)*
(B) *"wield" (line 7) and "falsification" (line 17)*
(C) *"conjectures" (line 16) and "truck with" (line 19)*
(D) *"extremism" (line 20) and "implausible" (line 24)*
(E) *"naïve" (line 35) and "errors" (line 42)*

[37]See Appendix C, page 100.

The correct answer is (D), "extremism" (line 20) and "implausible" (line 24). As the term "extremism" is used in line 20, it applies to the authors of the thesis mentioned in line 56, and thus indirectly to the thesis itself.[38] In line 24, the author uses the term "implausible" to characterize one aspect of the thesis, its rejection of a traditional belief. Taken together, these two words reveal a strongly negative attitude on the part of the author toward the thesis at issue. By contrast, in the incorrect answer choices, at least one of the terms presented, though it may reveal an attitude of the author's, does not apply to the thesis in line 56. For example, one of the incorrect answer choices is "naïve" (line 35) and "errors" (line 42). Both words are good candidates for indicating attitude, and both are used by the author to express an attitude. However, when you look at line 35, you discover that the author uses "naïve" to characterize a view that is an extreme opposite of the thesis at issue, and so does not express the author's attitude toward the thesis itself. Having discovered this much, you know that you can rule out this answer choice, whatever it is that "errors" applies to.

QUESTIONS ABOUT THE SIGNIFICANCE OF ADDITIONAL INFORMATION

Good readers read critically. That is to say, as they read the particular case an author makes for taking a certain position, they do not just passively take in what is on the page. Rather, they evaluate the plausibility, coherence, and strength of the claims and arguments advanced by the author. As they go along, they evaluate the strength of the author's case. They may think of objections to the way an author supports a position. Alternatively, they may think of things that the author hasn't mentioned that would have strengthened the author's case. Or they may think of questions to which they don't know the answer but that would be relevant questions to raise.

The test does not require you to think up considerations that would either strengthen or undercut the case an author has made for a position, but it does include questions that require you to recognize such considerations. You will be asked to determine whether new information strengthens or weakens a particular argument made in the passage. Often, the question will use the words **strengthen** or **weaken** themselves. But questions might also use analogous expressions such as to **support**, **bolster**, or **reinforce** a given claim or position; or to **undermine**, **challenge**, or **call into question** a given claim or position.

The following is an example of how a question might be phrased that requires you to recognize a difficulty with an explanation that has been proposed:

Which one of the following, if true, would most seriously undermine the explanation proposed by the author in the third paragraph?

(A) *A number of songbird species related to the canary have a shorter life span than the canary and do not experience neurogenesis.*
(B) *The brain size of several types of airborne birds with life spans similar to those of canaries has been shown to vary according to a two-year cycle of neurogenesis.*
(C) *Several species of airborne birds similar to canaries in size are known to have brains that are substantially heavier than the canary's brain.*
(D) *Individual canaries that have larger-than-average repertoires of songs tend to have better developed muscles for flying.*
(E) *Individual canaries with smaller and lighter brains than the average tend to retain a smaller-than-average repertoire of songs.*

Notice that the proviso "if true" means that you are told to treat each answer choice as if it is true, at least for the purposes of this question. You do not have to concern yourself with whether it is actually true. The explanation in the third paragraph to which the question refers is an explanation of a phenomenon called neurogenesis (the growth of new neurons) that has been observed in canaries:

A possible explanation for this continual replacement of nerve cells may have to do with the canary's relatively long life span and the requirements of flight. Its brain would have to be substantially larger and heavier than might be feasible for flying if it had to carry all the brain cells needed to process and retain all the information gathered over a lifetime.[39]

In other words, neurogenesis is held to be explained by the hypothesized need to keep the canaries' brains small and light so that the birds can fly. This explanation would have to be abandoned, or at least greatly modified, if the correct answer, (C), were true: "Several species of airborne birds similar to canaries in size are known to have brains that are substantially heavier than the canary's brain." In other words, assuming that this answer choice is true, it seems unlikely that canaries would have any difficulty flying even if their brains were a good bit heavier than they are. In that case, the requirements of flight would not

[38]See Appendix C, page 101.
[39]See Appendix C, page 102.

appear to be what dictates the small brain size in canaries and thus could not be invoked to explain neurogenesis, the mechanism by which canary brains are kept small.

In this example, the explanation depended on a certain supposition's being true. The additional information suggests that this supposition might well not be true. In other questions that ask about what would weaken or strengthen something in the passage, the additional information given in the correct answer might be related to the passage in other ways. For example, the additional information might suggest that something is true that would have been predicted given what the passage says, thereby strengthening the case made in the passage. Or it might tell you that something that would have been predicted given what the passage says doesn't, or isn't likely to, happen, in which case the argument advanced in the passage would be weakened. Or it might suggest that a generalization that the passage relied on does not hold up in the particular case under consideration. Or it might suggest that a claim made in the passage is unlikely to be true.

What you have to keep in mind is that what you're looking for is information that has an impact on the plausibility of the position, explanation, claim, evidence, and so on that the question specifically asks you about.

It is not enough that a piece of information is about something that the passage is concerned with or even about the particular thing that the question is about. The correct answer has to have a real effect on the strength of the position being asked about.

On the other hand, the correct answer does not have to conclusively establish or definitively refute the position being asked about. Given that these questions ask about what would **strengthen** or **weaken** something said in the passage, it is enough for the correct answer to increase (for **strengthen** questions) or decrease (for **weaken** questions) the likelihood that the argument or position in question is right.

COMPARATIVE READING

Since June 2007, the LSAT Reading Comprehension section has included a variant of Reading Comprehension called Comparative Reading. It is similar in many ways to single-passage Reading Comprehension, albeit with one major difference: Comparative Reading questions are based on two shorter passages instead of one longer passage.

Every LSAT Reading Comprehension section contains four sets of questions, one of which is a Comparative Reading

set. Together, the two passages in a Comparative Reading set are of roughly the same length as one Reading Comprehension passage.

Most of the questions that follow a Comparative Reading passage pair concern both passages taken together. The fundamental reading skills you need to answer such questions are similar to those required by single-passage Reading Comprehension questions. Even though the underlying skills are basically the same, however, the application of single-passage Reading Comprehension questions to two passages at once can sometimes lead to questions that look and feel very different (see the "How to Approach Comparative Reading Questions" section below). Some questions in Comparative Reading sets might ask about only one or the other of the two passages. Since these questions deal with only one passage, they are in essence identical to single-passage Reading Comprehension questions.

Comparative reading sets reflect some important aspects of law school work, which requires the ability to understand and synthesize arguments from multiple texts. Law students must be able to identify similarities and differences between facts, arguments, and principles found in different texts, and to synthesize principles from different instances or cases. They must be able to apply principles from one text to new situations in a different text on the basis of significant analogies between them, or to distinguish cases on the basis of disanalogies. And they must be able to recognize the relevance of different cases, decisions, and arguments to each other or to new or hypothetical situations. These tasks involve skills of comparison, contrast, synthesis, and generalization applied to multiple texts. The purpose of Comparative Reading is to assess this set of skills more directly than single-passage Reading Comprehension does.

What Comparative Reading Passage Pairs Look Like

The two passages in a Comparative Reading set—labeled "Passage A" and "Passage B"—discuss the same topic or related topics. These topics fall into the same broad categories used in single-passage Reading Comprehension: humanities, natural sciences, social sciences, and issues related to the law. Like single-passage Reading Comprehension passages, Comparative Reading passages are complex and generally involve argument. The two passages in a set are typically written by two different authors, and they are usually independent of each other—in other words, neither author is responding directly to the other.

To answer Comparative Reading questions, you first need to be able to understand the type of relationship that exists between the passages. So before we begin our discussion of the types of questions you will be likely to see in Comparative Reading sets, it's worth taking a look at a few of the general types of relationship between passages that you might encounter. These include the following:

- **Passages with competing or conflicting positions:** The passages in such Comparative Reading sets seek to answer the same question or address the same problem, but they take different positions. Sometimes the two passages take competing, though not necessarily contradictory, positions. And sometimes the arguments made by the two authors are in direct opposition to each other. For example, in one Comparative Reading set, passage A raises concerns regarding the spread in North America of an invasive plant species called purple loosestrife, and it calls for a coordinated control program.[40] Passage B, meanwhile, argues that what is threatened by purple loosestrife is not "nature," but rather the economic exploitation of nature through hunting, recreation, and so on. Among the skills tested by the questions that usually follow pairs like this is the ability to infer which specific claims the two authors would disagree about, and which claims they would agree on despite their overall strong disagreement (there are usually at least a few points of agreement even in texts that disagree strongly).

- **Passages that cover a topic in a nonconflicting way:** The passages in these Comparative Reading sets take different, though typically related, approaches to the same general topic. Unlike the passages in the first category described above, however, the arguments made in these passages do not conflict or compete with each other. Instead, the arguments in the two passages typically complement each other in some way. For example, both passages in a second Comparative Reading set discuss the early twentieth-century American author Willa Cather.[41] The two passages are similar in that both discuss her "impressionistic" narrative technique. But they differ in that passage A compares her narrative technique to that of nineteenth-century Russian author Ivan Turgenev, while passage B asserts that Cather's narrative style anticipates the literary theory of "narratology," which came to prominence in the 1960s. So the two passages do not disagree in any way; rather, the information provided by each complements the information provided by the other, and together they provide a fuller account of the narrative technique

developed by Cather. Among the skills tested by the questions that usually follow pairs like this is that of applying ideas developed in one text to the contents of a related text with a different approach.

Note also that within this category, there are two specific subcategories of relationships that are important enough to warrant being discussed on their own:

- **Passages that make general and specific arguments about the same topic:** In this type of Comparative Reading pair, one passage discusses a subject in general terms, and the other passage addresses the same topic at a more specific level. In many cases, one passage articulates certain principles that should govern a particular activity, and the other passage describes or instantiates that activity in some detail. For example, in another Comparative Reading set, passage A is excerpted from a British government "White Paper" (that is, a government policy paper) arguing in favor of proposed new freedom of information legislation.[42] Passage B, on the other hand, states a general argument regarding the characteristics any good freedom of information legislation must have. Among the skills tested by the questions that usually follow pairs like this is the ability to understand the ways in which a set of particulars conforms, or fails to conform, to principles that are meant to govern such particulars.

- **Passages that are similar on the general level but different in their particular topics:** These sets typically involve two passages that do not cover the same topic on the level of particulars, but that make analogous arguments at a more abstract level. For example, in a Comparative Reading set concerned with the topic of writing, passage A discusses the poor quality of writing among professional historians, and passage B discusses poor writing in the legal profession.[43] On the level of particulars, then, the two passages discuss different professions. But at the same time they are addressing the same problem in the two professions, and, moreover, both passages describe efforts to reform writing in their respective professions by emphasizing the importance of narrative in good writing. Thus, on a more general level, the two passages are making parallel arguments. Among the skills tested by the questions that usually follow pairs like this is the ability to identify where two similar arguments overlap, and where they differ in their application of general principles to different particular cases.

---

[40]See Appendix C, page 103.
[41]See Appendix C, page 104.
[42]See Appendix C, page 105.
[43]See Appendix C, page 106.

One thing to bear in mind is that in Comparative Reading—as in single-passage Reading Comprehension—it is a good idea to try to determine the main point and primary purpose of each passage while you are reading it. Likewise, it is useful to identify, as much as you can, what kind of relationship the passages have to each other. Most Comparative Reading sets will have at least one question that asks directly about the main points and purposes of the two passages, as well as questions that ask about the relationship between the two passages. Moreover, even questions that do not ask about these global features directly will address characteristics of the two passages in ways that are shaped by the global features.

HOW TO APPROACH COMPARATIVE READING QUESTIONS

A Note About Terminology

Before starting our discussion of Comparative Reading questions, it will be useful to establish some terminology. The phrases *questions that ask about only one passage* and *questions that ask about both passages* are long and cumbersome, so shorthand ways of referring to them will help us avoid unnecessary repetition.

To that end, we will use the label "bridge questions" to refer to questions that ask about both passages taken together (since these questions build bridges, metaphorically speaking, between the two passages). In contrast, questions that ask about only one of the passages will be called "nonbridge questions."

The following discussion of Comparative Reading questions is divided into three sections. The first section will cover nonbridge questions. The second section will cover bridge questions in which the reading tasks closely resemble the tasks required by single-passage Reading Comprehension questions. The third, and most substantial, section on Comparative Reading questions will be devoted to a discussion of bridge questions that bear less resemblance to single-passage Reading Comprehension questions. As we said earlier, these questions still rely on basically the same fundamental reading skills as single-passage Reading Comprehension questions. Nonetheless, applying these skills to two passages sometimes results in questions that look and feel significantly different.

Nonbridge Questions

The most important thing to know about nonbridge questions is that they are, for all intents and purposes, identical to their counterparts in single-passage Reading Comprehension. They fall into the same question-type categories, and they function in essentially the same way.

They should therefore be approached in the same way as single-passage Reading Comprehension questions, as discussed above in the various sections concerned with questions in single-passage sets (see pages 47–60). Consequently, it is not necessary to add much to the discussion already found in that section. The advice already given in that section applies equally well to nonbridge questions. Let's take a look at two nonbridge questions that illustrate this point.

Both passages in a particular Comparative Reading set discuss "drilling muds," which are fluids used by the oil industry to aid in the drilling of oil wells.[44] Passage A discusses the specific functions of drilling muds as well as the various substances found in drilling muds. Passage B, meanwhile, discusses the impact of these fluids on ocean ecology when they are used in off-shore drilling. In particular, passage B distinguishes the level of ecological impact resulting from the release of two different kinds of drilling mud: water-based muds (WBMs) and oil-based muds (OBM). One question in this set asks, "According to passage B, one reason OBMs are potentially more environmentally damaging than WBMs is that OBMs" and the correct response is (A), "are slower to disperse." Passage B states this directly in lines 53–54; this question is therefore a textbook example of the question type that asks about what is stated in the passage (discussed on pages 49–53 in the section "Questions About What the Passages Say or Imply"). And again, what is most relevant here is that answering this question is essentially no different from answering questions of this type in single-passage Reading Comprehension sets.

Likewise, in another Comparative Reading set, both passages discuss how the term "minority" functions in the legal context.[45] The passages discuss how that term is defined in international law, and in individual nations' legal systems as well, and they point out that there is generally a lack of clarity in how the term is used in the legal context. Both passages also assert that this lack of clarity often poses a problem for minority groups seeking to gain recognition for their rights, and that this problem is particularly acute for the people known as the Roma (traditionally called Gypsies).

One question in the set asks, "Which one of the following most accurately expresses the main point of passage A?" The correct response is (E), "The absence of a clear, generally agreed-upon understanding of what constitutes a people, nation, or minority group is a problem, especially in relation to the Roma."

[44]See Appendix C, page 107.
[45]See Appendix C, page 108.

The task involved here—that of identifying the main point of a single passage that appears in a Comparative Reading set—is really no different from the task of identifying the main point of a single-passage Reading Comprehension passage. Granted, passages in Comparative Reading sets differ from single-passage Reading Comprehension passages in certain ways that might seem significant: Comparative Reading passages are shorter than single-passage Reading Comprehension passages, and they come paired with a related passage, something that is not true of single-passage Reading Comprehension passages, of course. But neither of these differences is ultimately germane to the task of identifying the main point of one of the passages in a Comparative Reading set. You find the main point of an individual Comparative Reading passage in the same way you find the main point of a single-passage Reading Comprehension passage—by identifying the thrust of the passage, the most important idea that the passage seeks to establish. (See pages 48–49 under "Questions About the Passage as a Whole" for a full discussion of how main point questions work in single-passage Reading Comprehension.)

The same point can be made about all nonbridge questions. Questions that ask about the meaning of a word or phrase in one passage in a Comparative Reading set are essentially identical to questions of that type in single-passage Reading Comprehension sets (see pages 53–54 under "Questions That Require Using Context to Refine Meaning"). Questions that ask you to infer what one of the two authors would agree with function in the same way as those question types in single-passage Reading Comprehension (see pages 49–53 under "Questions About What the Passage Says or Implies"). And so on.

Bridge Questions That Resemble Single-Passage Reading Comprehension Questions

Like nonbridge questions, bridge questions fit into the same question types as single-passage Reading Comprehension questions, and in many cases, bridge questions require reading tasks that are effectively the same as those required by the same question types in single-passage Reading Comprehension. The difference, of course, is that the reading skill involved is being applied to two passages simultaneously, rather than to just one passage. To see what we mean, consider the following examples.

A second question in the Comparative Reading set that discusses the term "minority" as it applies to the Roma[46] is a bridge question that focuses on a key word that both passages use. The question asks, "The term 'problematic' has which one of the following meanings in both passage A (line 19) and passage B (line 35)?" Several of the responses offer meanings that the word "problematic" could conceivably have in different contexts: (B) is "confusing and unclear," for example, and (E) is "theoretically incoherent." But it becomes clear from the surrounding context in both passages that (C), "resulting in difficulties," is the response that reflects the way the word is used by both authors.

The important point for the purposes of this discussion is that in connection with each passage considered separately, the task of construing the meaning of the word in question by using the surrounding context is precisely the same as the task required by the same question type in single-passage Reading Comprehension (see pages 53–54 under "Questions That Require Using Context to Refine Meaning" for a full discussion of how this question type works in Reading Comprehension). The primary way in which this particular question differs from similar questions in single-passage Reading Comprehension is that the task is performed twice here, once for each passage. The nature of the task itself does not change, however.

[46]See Appendix C, page 108.

NOTE. You might be wondering how you will recognize the difference between bridge questions that are like single-passage Reading Comprehension questions and those that represent more of a departure from single-passage Reading Comprehension. In other words, as you prepare for the test, how can you tell which bridge questions fall into which category?

The first thing to you should know is that you do not need to focus on this distinction, or even to be aware of it at all, in order to answer bridge questions correctly. Every bridge question can be answered on its own terms without reference to categories like the one being discussed here. We have brought up the distinction simply because it is useful for discussing bridge questions and how they work.

That said, there is a relatively easy way of telling which category individual bridge questions fall into. A bridge question that works like a single-passage Reading Comprehension question will typically ask its question in a way that's simply a variation on the kind of wording used in the corresponding question type in standard Reading Comprehension, as is the case in the example discussed above. (We say "a variation," of course, because the difference is that a bridge question will explicitly refer to "both passages," or to "passage A and passage B.") What bridge questions that represent a more significant departure from single-passage Reading Comprehension look like will become clearer in the next section.

For a second example, let's look at another question from the Comparative Reading set about drilling muds discussed on page 62 under "Nonbridge Questions."[47] Both passages discuss barite, an important ingredient in many drilling muds, but they each offer different pieces of information about it. This particular question asks, "Which one of the following is a characteristic of barite that is mentioned in both of the passages?" The correct response is (D), "It is a heavy mineral." And indeed, passage A describes barite as a "very heavy mineral" in line 15, while passage B describes it as a "powdered heavy mineral" in line 51. It is clear, then, that the task required by this question is essentially the same as that required by single-passage Reading Comprehension questions that ask about what the passage states or mentions.

This question also illustrates another important feature of many bridge questions. If the correct response to a bridge question like the one above is the one that applies to both passages, then the incorrect responses will obviously be those that do not apply to both passages. But the important thing to note is that many incorrect answers in these cases will be correct with respect to one or the other of the two passages, just not both. For example, in the above question concerning barite, response (D) states, "It is the most commonly used ingredient in drilling muds." This assertion is supported by lines 14–16 in passage A, but nothing like it is referred to or mentioned in passage B.

To sum up, then, questions like these essentially involve using the same reading skill that you would use in the corresponding Reading Comprehension question type, and using it in essentially the same way. The difference, again, is that the skill is applied twice. Consequently, the advice provided in the "How to Approach Reading Comprehension Questions" section applies to bridge questions like these as well.

Bridge Questions That Differ Significantly From Single-Passage Reading Comprehension Questions

The bridge questions in this category focus on *the relationship* between the two passages. In many cases, the questions in this group involve varieties of tasks that are not even possible unless there are two passages under consideration. To see what we mean, turn your attention back for a moment to the bridge questions we discussed in the previous section. As we noted above, those questions involved tasks that one could be asked to perform with respect to one passage: for example, the first question discussed in the previous section concerned the meaning of the word "problematic" as it is used in the two passages concerning the Roma. This is a question type, and a reading task, that you will find in many single-passage Reading Comprehension sets; as applied in the Comparative Reading set, the same task is performed twice.

In contrast, the current group of bridge questions involve tasks that you could not be asked to perform in a single-passage Reading Comprehension set. For example, in a Comparative Reading set concerned with the phenomenon of global warming,[48] one of the questions regarding the authors' views asks, "The author of passage A would be most likely to agree with which one of the following assertions from passage B?" The responses are all assertions that were actually made in passage B, and the correct response is, of course, the one that that author of passage A would accept as valid. This question will be discussed more fully below, but for now it suffices to point

[47]See Appendix C, page 107.
[48]See Appendix C, page 109.

out that this task—identifying which one of five assertions an author would agree with, when those assertions are all extracted from a *text written independently by a different author*—is one that could not be found in a single-passage Reading Comprehension set.

All of the questions discussed in the sections that follow share this characteristic: they involve tasks that in some fundamental way reflect relationships that emerge from the juxtaposition of two texts. In other words, these bridge questions capture a set of reading skills required by law school work that are not directly captured by other Reading Comprehension questions.

QUESTIONS ABOUT MAIN POINTS AND PRIMARY PURPOSES

Main Point Questions

Asking a bridge question about the main points of distinct passages is more complex than it might at first appear. This is because any two texts written by two different authors are likely to have distinct main points. When two authors with distinct interests, concerns, and knowledge bases independently produce two texts, even if they discuss the same topic, one would not expect that their texts would end up with the precisely the same argumentative thrust.

In other words, there is usually no correct answer for the question, "Which one of the following most accurately expresses the main point of both passages?" Nonetheless, the ability to understand the main points of two texts on related topics, and the ability to see how those main points relate to each other, is extremely important for high-level academic work involving multiple texts.

A good way of getting at this important skill in Comparative Reading sets, then, is by way of the notion that each passage seeks to answer a question. In other words, one way of understanding any text with a unified point and a central purpose is to see it as attempting to respond to a particular question. This is not to say that every author writes with some question consciously in mind (nor would we have any way of knowing whether that was the case, unless the author told us so explicitly). Rather, what we mean is that an interpretive device that readers can use to understand the main point or purpose of a passage is to identify the main question that the passage answers. Articulating the question the passage answers is a way of identifying both the broader context in which passage operates, and also the goal of the passage.

Because Comparative Reading pairs discuss similar or related topics, it is often the case that both passages can be characterized as seeking to answer the same question, even if they disagree on many important points. Asking readers to identify the question that both passages seek to answer is therefore a very concise and effective way of assessing the ability to understand how two complex passages relate to each other with respect to their main points. Two examples will illustrate what we mean.

First, let's look at the bridge main point question from a set in which both passages discuss the evolution of the human ability to make and enjoy music.[49] Passage A asserts that music makes use of the same neurological circuits as language. The author continues, "The primacy of language over music that we can observe today suggests that language, not music, was the primary function natural selection operated on." Therefore, the author concludes, music "most likely developed on the coattails of language," which means that it "had little adaptive value of its own." Passage B, in contrast, argues that human musical ability derives from "premusical mother-infant interactions" that are composed of musical elements such as pitch, rhythm, timbre, volume, and tempo. These interactions themselves provided an evolutionary advantage, according to passage B. The increase in hominid brain size, together with the narrowing of the birth canal due to bipedality, meant that hominid infants were born progressively earlier and more helpless. This in turn necessitated longer and better maternal care, and the emotional bonds formed through the mother-infant premusical interactions conferred a significant advantage in that respect. Finally, the neurological basis for these interactions forms the basis for the capacity to make and enjoy music. Thus, passage B concludes, the basic human capacity for music did in fact confer an evolutionary advantage.

The main point in this set reads as follows:

Both passages were written primarily in order to answer which one of the following questions?

(A) *What evolutionary advantage did larger brain size confer on early hominids?*
(B) *Why do human mothers and infants engage in bonding behavior that is composed of musical elements?*
(C) *What are the evolutionary origins of the human ability to make music?*
(D) *Do the human abilities to make music and to use language depend on the same neurological systems?*
(E) *Why are most people more adept at using language than they are at making music?*

The correct response is (C). Even though the two passages argue opposing points, they can still be understood as answering the same question. Indeed, the conflict between them consists precisely in their answering that question in opposing ways.

Primary Purpose Questions

In Comparative Reading sets whose passages are fairly similar, you may see bridge primary purpose questions that ask you to identify the purpose that is central to both passages. For example, consider the "drilling muds" Comparative Reading pair, discussed on page 62 under "Nonbridge Questions."[50] As was noted above, both of these passages discuss the composition of drilling muds. Moreover, both passages discuss certain properties of drilling muds: passage A discusses the properties that make them useful in oil-well drilling, while passage B discusses the specific components and properties that can make drilling muds more or less dangerous to ocean ecologies when released. The primary purpose question in this set reads,

A primary purpose of each of the passages is to

(A) *provide causal explanations for a type of environmental pollution*
(B) *describe the general composition and properties of drilling muds*
(C) *point out possible environmental impacts associated with oil drilling*
(D) *explain why oil-well drilling requires the use of drilling muds*
(E) *identify difficulties inherent in the regulation of oil-well drilling operations*

The correct response is (B). It is worth noting, by the way, that you will not encounter bridge primary purpose questions like this in many Comparative Reading passage pairs. If the two passages are quite similar in their content and their approach, as the drilling muds passages are, then you might very well see a question like this one. But if the passages diverge significantly in their content and approach, the situation is rather like that described in relation to main point questions above: there is no longer a single purpose that can be ascribed to both passages.

QUESTIONS ABOUT WHAT THE PASSAGES SAY OR IMPLY

For the most part, bridge questions about what the passages say are quite similar to questions of the same type in single-passage Reading Comprehension. Such questions often ask about something that is mentioned or

asserted in both passages, in which case the task is essentially the same as that in single-passage Reading Comprehension (see the "Bridge Questions That Resemble Single-Passage Reading Comprehension Questions" section on pages 63–64). One variant that you might encounter, however, asks you to identify something that is mentioned (or stated, asserted, etc.) in one passage, but not in the other. Questions like this focus on significant differences in what the two passages say (as opposed to differences in insignificant details). But although these questions ask about a difference in the contents of the two passages, they still work very much like single-passage Reading Comprehension questions in most respects. The rest of this section will therefore be devoted to a discussion of questions that focus on what the passages imply.

In Comparative Reading, most of the questions about what can be inferred from the passages deal with the views of the two authors. This makes sense inasmuch as drawing inferences regarding two independently written texts will naturally focus attention on the views of the authors who produced the texts. After all, the salient similarities and differences between the two texts derive from the different perspectives, interests, knowledge, and approaches of the two authors.

Inferences about the views of the two authors fall into three categories: inferences about things the two authors would agree on; inferences about things the two authors would disagree on; and inferences about the view one author would be likely to hold regarding some element in the other passage.

Questions About Things the Authors Would Agree On

Almost every Comparative Reading set will have at least one question that asks the following (or some variation on it): "The authors of the passages would be most likely to agree on which one of the following?" In some respects, this type of bridge question is quite similar to the corresponding question type in single-passage Reading Comprehension—you are being asked to identify something that one of the authors agrees with, and then you perform that task again with respect to the other passage. But in other key respects, this type of bridge question does in fact differ significantly from the single-passage Reading Comprehension version.

The task of identifying points of agreement between the authors of two distinct texts gets at something that is important and unique about Comparative Reading, and it reflects a high-level skill that is necessary for working with multiple texts. If you are able to understand where the

[50]See Appendix C, page 107.

authors of two passages agree, then you understand a lot about the two passages and how they relate to each other. An example will help illustrate what we mean. Let's look back again at the Comparative Reading set in which both passages seek to provide an explanation for the evolution of the human ability to make and enjoy music.[51] Passage A argues that humans' musical ability evolved "on the coattails" of language. The author writes,

> Given their shared neurological basis, it appears that music and language evolved together as brain size increased over the course of hominid evolution. But the primacy of language over music that we can observe today suggests that language, not music, was the primary function natural selection operated on.

In contrast, passage B argues that the human capacity for music is derived from premusical mother-infant interactions among early hominids. These interactions, which make use of musical elements such as pitch and rhythm, facilitated the formation of emotional bonds, which in turn promoted better maternal care. This better maternal care was itself made necessary by the combination of rapid increases in hominid brain size and bipedality, the latter of which resulted in a narrower birth canal; these factors resulted in hominid infants' being born progressively earlier and more helpless. Thus, the author concludes, the emotional bonds formed through the premusical interactions—"behavior whose neurological basis essentially constitutes the ability to make and enjoy music"—would have conferred a significant evolutionary advantage.

In other words, the two authors reach opposing conclusions regarding the evolutionary benefits of the human capacity for music. Nonetheless, one question in the set requires you to identify a significant point of agreement in their views:

> The authors would be most likely to agree on the answer to which one of the following questions regarding musical capacity in humans?
>
> (A) Does it manifest itself in some form in early infancy?
> (B) Does it affect the strength of mother-infant bonds?
> (C) Is it at least partly a result of evolutionary increases in brain size?
> (D) Did its evolution spur the development of new neurological systems?
> (E) Why does it vary so greatly among different individuals?

The correct response is (C). What this question illuminates is that while the explanations offered by the two authors conflict with each other, they also overlap in a way that is significant and perhaps unexpected at first: both explanations presume that the evolution of humans' musical capacity was intimately bound up with the rapid increase in hominid brain size. This is the sort of relationship that highly skilled readers are able to identify.

Questions About Things the Authors Would Disagree On

As the name of this category suggests, these questions can be regarded as the mirror image of the type of question we just discussed. Just as good readers are able to find points of agreement amidst points of disagreement between two texts, good readers are also able to identify points of disagreement amidst points of agreement.

An illustration of this type of question can be found in the Comparative Reading set that discusses global warming.[52] Passage A in this set holds that global warming is caused to a significant degree by human activity, while passage B argues that natural events appear to be a far more important factor in global warming. One question in the set reads,

> The authors of the two passages would be most likely to disagree over
>
> (A) whether or not any melting of the polar ice caps has occurred
> (B) whether natural events can cause changes in global climate conditions
> (C) whether warmer air temperatures will be likely to raise oceanic water temperatures
> (D) the extent to which natural climate variability is responsible for global warming
> (E) the extent to which global temperatures have risen in recent decades

The correct response is (D). One notable feature of this question is that the incorrect responses point to several matters on which the authors agree, despite their overall disagreement. They agree that the polar ice caps have experienced some melting (response A), that natural events can cause changes in global climate (B), and that warmer air temperatures will likely raise ocean temperatures (C). Neither passage provides any specific information about the extent to which global temperatures have risen in recent decades (E), but they agree that the earth has gotten warmer. So the passages give us is no reason to think that the authors would disagree about the extent of the warming. What they would disagree about, however, is the matter alluded to in the correct response: the extent to which natural climate variability is responsible for global warming. This task reflects an important, high-level skill: the ability to identify significant points of both agreement and disagreement among multiple texts. Note, by the way, that the correct response in this example goes to the heart of the dispute between the two authors. This will not always be the case—many questions about points of disagreement between the authors will focus on matters that, while they are important, are not so closely linked to the central dispute in the pair.

Questions About the Way One Author Would Be Likely to View an Element in the Other Passage

Questions belonging to this final group of bridge questions regarding the views of the authors do not ask you to compare the views of the two authors and find points of agreement or disagreement. Instead, these questions ask you to draw inferences regarding what one of the authors would be likely to think regarding something found in the other passage. This type of question assesses the ability to understand the principles or positions to which an author is committed, and to apply them to some content outside of the author's text (in this case, the other passage).

An example of this question type can be found in the Comparative Reading pair that discusses freedom of information systems.[53] As discussed above (see page 61 under "What Comparative Reading Passage Pairs Look Like"), passage A in this set argues in favor of a proposed new freedom of information legislative package. In the course of doing so, passage A describes several of the shortcomings of the predecessor to the proposed legislation, which was known as the Code of Practice on Access to Government Information. Passage B, meanwhile, articulates a series of principles determining what characteristics a good freedom of information system should have. One question in this set reads,

If the author of passage B were to read passage A, he or she would be most likely to draw which one of the following conclusions regarding matters addressed in passage A?

(A) *The Code of Practice did not allow sufficient public access to information.*
(B) *It would have been premature for the previous government to have enacted statutory measures to guarantee freedom of information.*

(C) *The measures recommended by the current government are unnecessarily complex.*
(D) *Freedom of information laws ought not to allow sensitive material to be deleted from any document before disclosure of the document.*
(E) *The current government's proposed legislation depends too heavily on the questionable assumption that "public interest" can be clearly defined.*

The correct answer is (A). The Code of Practice, as it is described in passage A, fails to conform to several of the principles listed in passage B. For example, passage B states that there must be a presumption in favor of disclosure (lines 45–47), whereas the Code of Practice, as described in passage A, encouraged a "category-based" approach in which "whole classes of information or records are protected against disclosure" (lines 27–29). Similarly, passage B argues that exemptions should be limited to cases in which "it can be shown that disclosure of the particular piece of information withheld would cause harm to one or more [public] interests" (lines 54–57), whereas according to passage A, the Code of Practice "contains too many exemptions—more than any of the main statutory freedom of information regimes elsewhere in the world" (lines 19–21). All of the evidence thus supports the conclusion that the author of passage B would regard the Code of Practice as a freedom of information system that did not allow sufficient public access to government information. Answering this question correctly depends on the ability to understand the principles articulated in passage B, and to apply them to the information in passage A.

QUESTIONS THAT FOCUS ON THE RELATIONSHIP BETWEEN THE PASSAGES

Law school work requires the ability to read multiple related texts in conjunction, and to recognize and understand the kinds of relationships in which those texts stand. Do the arguments and evidence offered in one text support those in a second text, or do they undermine the case made in that other text? Do the points made in one text conform to the principles articulated in a second text, or do they violate those principles? The relevance of these skills to the task of determining whether a lower court decision conforms to a precedent established in a superior court decision, for example, should be evident.

Accordingly, in Comparative Reading sets you will often encounter bridge questions that ask you to identify what kind relationship exists between the two passages. One example of this type of question can be found in the

[53]See Appendix C, page 105.

Comparative Reading set whose topic is a proposed freedom of information legislative package in the United Kingdom.[54] As we noted in the previous section, passage A argues in favor of the proposed new legislation, while passage B makes a more general argument regarding the characteristics that freedom of information legislation should have. In other words, passage B articulates a set of principles that are meant to guide the development of legislation like that proposed in passage A. An important reading task in this case, then, is that of assessing how well the proposed legislation in passage A conforms to the principles articulated in passage B. One question in this sets reads:

Which one of the following most accurately describes a way in which the two passages are related to each other?

(A) *Passage A contains reasoning of a kind that passage B suggests is fallacious.*

(B) *Passage B presupposes that information given in passage A regarding specific events is accurate.*

(C) *Passage A contains an explanation that, if valid, helps to resolve a paradox suggested in passage B.*

(D) *If all of the claims made in passage A are true, then some of the claims made in passage B are false.*

(E) *If the assertions made in passage B are valid, they strengthen the position expressed in passage A.*

If you read this pair of passages carefully, you will notice that the provisions described in passage A generally satisfy the requirements stated in passage B. Passage A argues in favor of the new government's proposed legislation by pointing to alleged flaws in the previous freedom of information system and pledging that the new regime would avoid those problems. The problems identified correspond quite closely to pitfalls identified in passage B, and the proposed new policies coincide quite well with the recommendations in passage B. Thus, the correct response is (E).

Another variety of bridge question about the relationship between the passages is concerned not so much with how the passages might impact each other, but rather with how the passages compare to each other in their general approach or orientation. For example, consider the organization question associated with the Comparative Reading pair that discusses purple loosestrife.[55] One striking feature of this pair of passages is that while the two passages are based on sources that were written independently of each other, passage B reads almost as though it had been written as a direct response to passage A. This is because the author of passage B is criticizing a general stance that passage A embodies nearly perfectly. Passage A, on the other hand, makes a straightforward case for taking measures to control purple loosestrife, without concerning itself with the views of those who might oppose such measures, like the author of passage B. (This is not to suggest that the author of passage A is unaware of the views of opponents of the position taken in passage A, but simply that the author of passage A does not address those views in this particular text.) Thus, while passage A says little about the kind of position taken in passage B, passage B has much to say about the kinds of views expressed in passage A. The following question in this set gets at the ability to draw conclusions like this:

Which one of the following is true about the relationship between the two passages?

(A) *Passage A presents evidence that directly counters claims made in passage B.*

(B) *Passage B assumes what passage A explicitly argues for.*

(C) *Passage B displays an awareness of the arguments touched on in passage A, but not vice versa.*

(D) *Passage B advocates a policy that passage A rejects.*

(E) *Passage A downplays the seriousness of claims made in passage B.*

The correct response here is (C).

QUESTIONS THAT REQUIRE THE RECOGNITION OF ANALOGOUS PATTERNS

Bridge questions that focus on analogous patterns come in two main varieties: questions that require you to recognize elements within the two passages that are in some way analogous to each other, and questions that require you to recognize a relationship between a pair of hypothetical documents that is analogous to the relationship between the two passages. Both varieties assess the ability to perceive analogies that exist between independently produced texts.

Analogous Elements Within the Passages
Often two texts discussing the same topic or related topics will argue certain points in analogous ways. This is likely to be so if they make arguments that agree on important points, but it may be true even if in the end the two texts disagree strongly in their main conclusions. One of the tasks performed by skilled readers is that of recognizing when texts by different authors coincide in their approach—in the claims they make, in the evidence they use, or in the way they use their evidence.

An example of a question that focuses on analogous elements can be found in the Comparative Reading set in which the two passages make parallel arguments concerning the poor quality of writing in a particular profession—academic history in passage A, and the law in passage B.[56] Both passages discuss efforts aimed at improving the writing in their respective professions by encouraging an increased emphasis on narrative. In a broad sense, then, one can say that these two passages are themselves analogous to each other in their arguments. One key element in understanding analogous arguments fully is the ability to perceive all of the particular points at which the analogy is maintained and developed, and to distinguish those from points that are not analogous. (In even the most elaborate and detailed analogies, there are points at which the correspondence is not maintained. This is because analogies exist only between things that are different in some way. Two things that are perfectly analogous in every possible way are not actually analogous; they are identical.)

In the Comparative Reading pair about writing, then, passage A asserts, "Historians require undergraduates to read scholarly monographs that sap the vitality of history." The author's point, of course, is that the problem with writing in academic history is that historians write in a way that drains the life out of history and makes for terribly dry, dull reading. The author continues by suggesting that historians learn this approach in their professional training in graduate school, charging that historians "visit on students what was visited on them in graduate school." One question in this set asks you to identify an element in passage B that plays a role that is analogous to the role played by the reference to scholarly monographs in passage A:

> The phrase "scholarly monographs that sap the vitality of history" in passage A (lines 6–7) plays a role in that passage's overall argument that is most analogous to the role played in passage B by which one of the following phrases?

(A) "Writing is at the heart of the lawyer's craft" (line 29)
(B) "Conformity is a virtue, creativity suspect, humor forbidden, and voice mute" (lines 37–38)
(C) "Lawyers write as they see other lawyers write" (line 39)
(D) "every case has at its heart a story" (line 46)
(E) Still, even mere awareness of the value of narrative could perhaps serve as an important corrective" (lines 57–59)

The correct answer is (B). This question is fairly easy. Nonetheless, answering the question correctly requires the ability to recognize not only that these two statements are similar to each other in their tone and in what they say, but also that they fit into the overall arguments in the two passages in analogous ways. Just as passage A suggests that it is the graduate training of historians that leads them to write in the way they do, passage B asserts, "Writing is at the heart of the lawyer's craft, and so, like it or not, we who teach the law inevitably teach aspiring lawyers how lawyers write." The results: according to passage A, "scholarly monographs that sap the vitality of history," and according to passage B, "Conformity is a virtue, creativity suspect, humor forbidden, and voice mute."

Analogy to Another Pair of Documents

A skill that is centrally important for reading two high-level texts together is the ability to perceive the kind of relationship in which the two passages in their entirety stand with respect to each other. One approach to this skill is found in questions that ask directly about the type of relationship the two passages have (discussed in the previous section, pages 69–70). Another approach is found in analogous pattern questions. In these questions, you are not asked to identify the response that best describes the relationship. Instead you are given descriptions of five pairs of hypothetical documents, and you are asked to identify the pair that stands in a relationship that is most analogous to the relationship between the passages in the Comparative Reading pair. The important thing to remember is that recognizing the analogous case requires you to perceive and understand the relationship between the passages.

One example of this type of question can be found in the set that discusses global warming.[57] As we discussed earlier under "Questions About Things the Authors Would Disagree On" (see page 67), both passages in this pair agree that global temperatures have risen in the past few decades. Passage A argues that there is now conclusive evidence that human activity is a primary factor in this warming trend. Passage B does not deny that human activity may be a factor, but it downplays the imprtance of human activity and asserts that natural events appear to be a far more important factor. Thus the two passages agree that there is a trend that calls for explanation, but they explain the trend in different ways. One question in this set reads:

[56]See Appendix C, page 106.
[57]See Appendix C, page 109.

The relationship between passage A and passage B is most analogous to the relationship between the documents described in which one of the following?

(A) a research report that raises estimates of damage done by above-ground nuclear testing; an article that describes practical applications for nuclear power in the energy production and medical fields

(B) an article arguing that corporate patronage biases scientific studies about the impact of pollution on the ozone layer; a study suggesting that aerosols in the atmosphere may counteract damaging effects of atmospheric carbon dioxide on the ozone layer

(C) an article citing evidence that the spread of human development into pristine natural areas is causing catastrophic increases in species extinction; an article arguing that naturally occurring cycles of extinction are the most important factor in species loss

(D) an article describing the effect of prolonged drought on crop production in the developing world; an article detailing the impact of innovative irrigation techniques in water-scarce agricultural areas

(E) a research report on crime and the decline of various neighborhoods from 1960 to 1985; an article describing psychological research on the most important predictors of criminal behavior

The two documents described in response (C) stand in a relationship of agreeing on the existence of a trend, but disagreeing on the cause of that trend. Response (C) is therefore the correct answer.

Note also that some questions of this type use titles to represent the hypothetical documents, rather than descriptions of the documents. For example, consider the set that discusses freedom of information systems.[58] As we saw earlier (see page 61 under "What Comparative Reading Passage Pairs Look Like"), passage A argues in favor of a proposed freedom of information legislative package that is intended to correct the shortcomings of its predecessor, and passage B describes a set of principles that define what a good freedom of information system should look like. The last question in the set reads:

Based on what can be inferred from their titles, the relationship between which one of the following pairs of documents is most analogous to the relationship between passage A and passage B?

(A) "What the Previous Management of the Midtown Health Club Left Undone"
"The New Management of the Crescent Restaurant Has Some Bad Policies"

(B) "A List of Grievances by Tenants of Garden Court Apartments"
"Why the Grievances of the Garden Court Apartments Tenants Are Unfounded"

(C) "How We Plan to Improve the Way in Which This Restaurant Is Managed"
"Standards of Good Restaurant Management"

(D) "Three Alternative Proposals for Our New Advertising Campaign"
"Three Principles to Be Followed in Developing an Effective Sales Team"

(E) "Detailed Instructions for Submitting a Formal Grievance to the Committee"
"Procedures for Adjudicating Grievances"

The correct response is (C). Response (C) is the only one that combines a document in which a proposal for improving how a specific enterprise is approached with a document that states general principles for conducting that type of enterprise. Other than the fact that the hypothetical documents in it are represented by their titles, this variant functions in the same way as questions that use descriptions of the documents.

QUESTIONS ABOUT AUTHORS' ATTITUDES

Bridge questions concerning authors' attitudes fall into two subcategories: questions that compare the attitudes displayed by the two authors, and questions that ask about the attitude one author has (or would be likely to have) toward a claim or argument made in the other passage.

Comparisons of Authors' Attitudes

Questions of this type ask about the attitudes displayed by the two authors, but not by asking for a direct description of the two authors' attitudes. Instead, if the authors' display attitudes toward their topics that differ in some way, as they usually do, you might be asked to identify how they are different. For example, the bridge attitude question in the freedom of information set reads:

Passage A differs from passage B in that passage A displays an attitude that is more

(A) partisan
(B) tentative
(C) analytical
(D) circumspect
(E) pessimistic

As we discussed above (see page 61), passage A argues in favor of a proposed new freedom of information legislative package, while passage B lays out principles that the

---

author believes should apply to any freedom of information system. In other words, while the author of passage A is taking a side in a debate, the author of passage B has no stake in any side of the debate, or any other debate, for that matter. Thus the correct response is (A) "partisan." Note that this question focuses on a difference between the attitudes of the two authors that is fairly subtle, but it is nonetheless the kind difference that could have a significant impact on the interpretation of two texts. An important reading skill is the ability to perceive such differences and put them to use in interpreting texts.

The Attitude One Author Has (Or Would Be Likely to Have) Toward Something in the Other Passage

Some bridge attitude questions focus not on how the attitudes of the two authors would compare, but rather on the attitude one author shows toward an idea or argument discussed in the other passage. (Or, if we do not have evidence that the author is already aware of that idea or argument, the question will ask about the attitude the author would be likely to have.) An example of this type of bridge attitude question can be found in the set that discusses purple loosestrife.[59] As we discussed earlier under "What Comparative Reading Passage Pairs Look Like" (see page 61), passage A argues that the invasive plant purple loosestrife poses a serious threat to North American wetlands ecosystems, while passage B is quite critical, and even scornful, of that position. Another question in the set reads:

Which one of the following most accurately describes the attitude expressed by the author of passage B toward the overall argument represented by passage A?

(A) *enthusiastic agreement*
(B) *cautious agreement*
(C) *pure neutrality*
(D) *general ambivalence*
(E) *pointed skepticism*

Given the sharply critical stance taken by the author of passage B, the correct response is (E) "pointed skepticism."

By the way, even though we have no evidence that the author of passage B has read passage A, it is clear from the argument in passage B that he or she is well aware of the type of argument advanced in passage A. Thus the question asks about the author's attitude toward "the overall argument represented by passage A."

QUESTIONS ABOUT AUTHORS

Another type of bridge question focuses on what can be inferred about the authors themselves. Typically, these questions focus on the authors' professional relationship to their topic. For example, if the topic in a Comparative Reading pair is a legal one, the question might be whether the authors of the passages are lawyers, judges, or outside observers.

An example from the Comparative Reading set concerned with the quality of professional writing[60] will help illustrate this question type. As discussed above (see page 70), the authors in this pair discuss the poor quality of writing in two professions: academic history and the legal profession. Both passages provide clear indications of their authors' relationships to these professions. The author of passage A writes, "The perniciousness of the historiographic approach became fully evident to me when I started teaching." Moreover, in the second paragraph, the author lists several topics offered at an academic history conference, and he or she concludes by saying, "At meetings of historians, we still encounter very few historians telling stories or moving audiences to smiles, chills, or tears." Passage B is even more direct and explicit: in line 30, the author uses the first person in referring to "we who teach the law." One question in this set reads,

The passages most strongly support which one of the following inferences regarding the authors' relationships to the professions they discuss?

(A) *Neither author is an active member of the profession that he or she discusses.*
(B) *Each author is an active member of the profession he or she discusses.*
(C) *The author of passage A is a member of the profession discussed in that passage, but the author of passage B is not a member of either of the professions discussed in the passages.*
(D) *Both authors are active members of the profession discussed in passage B.*
(E) *The author of passage B, but not the author of passage A, is an active member of both of the professions discussed in the passages.*

The correct response is (B). Relatively few Comparative Reading passage pairs will have this type of question, because not all of them provide such clear indications of what relationships their authors have to their topics. But the ability to detect these indications when they are available, and to make use of them to aid in comprehension as well, is an important reading skill. For instance, consider how different the Comparative Reading pair we just discussed would have been if we had evidence that either or both of the authors were not members of the professions they discuss, but simply interested outsiders.

---

[59]See Appendix C, page 103.
[60]See Appendix C, page 106.

APPENDIX A: USING DIAGRAMS IN ANSWERING ANALYTICAL REASONING QUESTIONS

Most people find that in answering Analytical Reasoning questions, diagrams can be very useful. Diagrams not only help you visualize the basic structure of the possible outcomes for a set of questions, they can also make clear what you can infer about the possible outcomes.

BASIC ABBREVIATIONS

The first step in answering Analytical Reasoning questions is to get a clear idea of what is specified in the passage on which a set of questions is based. After carefully reading the passage, it's generally a good idea to follow these two steps:

- Abbreviate the elements specified in the passage using their initials, and list them all, including any that aren't specifically mentioned in the conditions.

- Write out shorthand representations of the conditions.

In order to write out shorthand representations of the conditions, you'll want to have some handy abbreviations at the ready when you take the test. It's not usually a good idea to wait until test day to try to work out on the fly a system for representing the conditions. It doesn't matter what form your representations take, as long as they are clear and meaningful to you. If you're familiar with symbols used in computer programming or formal logic, by all means use those symbols. But don't worry if you're not familiar with those kinds of symbol systems—you can simply come up with your own. Don't assume that the suggestions provided in this appendix are always the best way or the only way to approach diagramming. Feel free to expand, simplify, or alter what you see here. When working with paper and pencil, you can use the space on the page in creative ways: use arrows, draw lines linking elements, cross things out, put elements above and below each other, or use brackets, lines, boxes, and circles.

What sorts of relationships and operations will you need to represent? Here are some that commonly occur in Analytical Reasoning:

- Fixed ordering (for example, "first" or "sixth")

- Relative ordering (for example, "earlier than" or "immediately before")

- Assignment to or inclusion in a group

- Conditionals ("if–then")

- Negation ("not")

- Conjunction ("and")

- Disjunction ("or")

Fixed Ordering
Many sets of questions involve ordering relations. These elements include fixed ordering , such as *Tracy must speak third*. You might, for example, represent this sort of relation by following the named element's initial with the appropriate number, perhaps enclosed in parentheses, or by adding a subscript to the element's initial:

$$T3 \qquad T(3) \qquad T_3$$

Another alternative for this particular example would be to use two underscores followed by the element's initial like this:

$$\_ \ \_ \ T$$

Relative Ordering
Some ordering conditions involve relative ordering of two or more named elements. For example, you might have a condition such as *Flag Street must be repaired at some time before River Road*, which you might abbreviate like this:

$$F..R$$

or maybe like this:

$$F < R$$

You'll also want a way to represent cases where two elements appear consecutively in a fixed order relative to one another. Suppose you have a condition like *X must be immediately before Y*. You might represent this as:

$$XY$$

Another type of relative ordering you'll encounter is strict adjacency, as in *The pharmacy must be next to the medical office*. Note that in a case like this, the relative order of the two elements themselves is not fixed. In this particular example, for instance, it doesn't matter whether the pharmacy appears earlier in the row of buildings than the medical center or later—all that matters is that no other building comes between the pharmacy and the medical center. To represent that elements must be adjacent to each other, but that their order relative to one another is not fixed, you might use an abbreviation like this:

P/M

or maybe this:

P∫M

Some other ordering conditions you're likely to encounter include cases where two elements must be separated by a fixed number of other elements or by at least some number of other elements. Suppose, for example, that you have a condition like *Exactly one day separates the day on which Juan works and the day on which Martha works*. This might be represented as:

J|M_M|J

Here, a vertical line is used to represent "or," "J|M" is used to represent "Juan or Martha," "M|J" is used to represent "Martha or Juan," and an underscore is used to represent "exactly one day." Note that the relative order of Juan and Martha is *not* specified in this condition. It could be that Juan works on an earlier day than Martha, but it could just as well be that Martha works on an earlier day than Juan. The only thing specified in the condition is that exactly one day comes between the days on which these two people work.

Now let's consider a case in which the condition you're trying to represent is somewhat similar to the one we just looked at but is different in a crucial respect. This time, suppose you have a condition like *At least one painting must be between R and T*. This might be represented as follows, where an underscore is flanked by leading and trailing dots to show that there has to be one painting between R and T but there might also be others as well:

R|T.._..T|R

Again, the relative order of the two named elements mentioned in the condition is *not* specified. It could be that R is earlier in the sequence of paintings than T, but it could just as well be that T is earlier in the sequence than R. All that the condition specifies is that at least one other painting comes between these two paintings.

Assignment to or Inclusion in a Group

Many sets of questions involve conditions that group elements together. Suppose the passage for a set of questions involves assigning people to committees. This passage might include a condition that specifies that a specific person must be assigned to a specific committee—for example, *Kahn must be on the grants committee*, which you might represent like this:

G:K

or like this:

K_G

Another type of grouping condition is one that involves two or more of the named elements. For example, you might have a condition such as *Liu and Miller must be on the same committee as each other*. Some of the ways you might represent this would be by listing the people's initials one after the other, by enclosing them together in parentheses or a circle, or maybe by giving them a common subscript:

LM   (LM) L_cM_c

Conditionals

Conditional statements specify what is the case if something else is true. A typical conditional is of the form *If X then Y*. There are other equivalent wordings, too. See the section "Conditional Statements" in A Guide to Analytical Reasoning Questions on pages 15–17 for a discussion of the different forms that conditional statements can take.

One way to represent a conditional statement is to use an arrow to indicate "if–then." For example, a condition such as *If the treasurer is seated at table 2, then the president must be seated at table 1* might be represented like this:

$T_2 \rightarrow P_1$

Negation

Statements that include negation are used to indicate what is *not* the case. For example, instead of having a condition that specifies that a particular task must be performed earlier than another, you might have a condition that specifies that the particular task *cannot* be performed earlier than the other. Or instead of having a condition that specifies that two particular people must be on the same team as each other, you might have a condition that specifies that those two people *cannot* be on the same team as each other. You can represent negation by adding a symbol such as * or ^ or ~ in front of other representations you've decided on. For example, suppose that you've decided to represent a condition such as *Jones must attend the projects meeting like this*:

J_P

Then you might represent the negative analog of that condition—*Jones cannot attend the projects meeting*—in any of the following ways:

$*J_P$ $^\wedge J_P$ $\sim J_P$

Here's another example. If you represent a condition such as *If Q speaks fourth, then T must speak fifth like this*:

$Q_4 \rightarrow T_5$

Then you might represent a condition such as *If Q speaks fourth, then T cannot speak fifth like this*:

$Q_4 \rightarrow {}^\wedge T_5$

Conjunction

In English, conjunction is normally represented as "and."* Here are a few examples of conditions that involve conjunction:

Both X and Y must be selected.

Pei attends the technology meeting, and Quinn attends the sales meeting.

Maria and Steve must both perform earlier than Tony.

In the first of these cases, you don't need any symbol to represent "and." All you need here is something like this:

XY

or this:

(XY)

In the second case, you might represent each of the two conjoined statements separately, as two separate conditions, like this:

P_T

Q_S

or you might join the two statements with a symbol representing "and," such as + or &:

$P_T + Q_S$ $P_T \& Q_S$

The third case is an interesting one. What it's saying is that Maria must perform earlier than Tony and that Steve must perform earlier than Tony. So you could represent this condition as if it were two separate conditions, like this:

M..T

S..T

That would be all right, but it doesn't strongly capture the fact that Tony has to perform later than both Maria and Steve. You might think that a representation like this would be better:

M&S..T

The problem with this representation, however, is that it doesn't strongly capture the fact that it doesn't matter whether Maria performs earlier or later than Steve, nor does it capture the fact that there might be other people who perform between Maria and Steve. If you want a representation that captures all of the facts clearly, you might prefer a representation like this:

M|S..S|M..T

Here, "M|S..S|M..T" is used as an abbreviation for "M..S..T or S..M..T." This representation immediately tells you that an acceptable order has either Maria or Steve, and later either Steve or Maria, and then Tony later still.

Disjunction

In English, disjunction is represented by the word "or." We just saw one way you could represent "or": use a vertical line ("|") between the two elements or statements that are disjoint. In the example we just looked at, "Maria or Steve" could be represented as:

M|S

One thing to be careful about, though, is that the English word "or" is ambiguous: *X or Y* can mean "X or Y but not both" or it can mean "X and/or Y." The former meaning is sometimes referred to as "exclusive or," the latter as "nonexclusive or." In many cases when "or" appears in a condition, the context of the passage ensures that "or" can only be interpreted as "exclusive or." For example, in a passage in which the task is to assign each of a set of

---

*Another English word that represents conjunction is "but." For example, *The petunias must be planted in flower bed 1 but the marigolds cannot be planted there.*

individuals to exactly one position, the "or" in a condition such as *Quentin must be assigned to the third or fourth position* can only be interpreted as "exclusive or": Quentin must be assigned to the third position or to the fourth position, *but not to both.*

In cases where the context does not help determine which meaning of "or" is intended, the wording of a condition will make it clear whether you should assume that "or" is to be understood as exclusive or nonexclusive. When "exclusive or" is intended, the condition will specify "but not both" as, for example, in *The committee must include Saito or Williams but not both.* When "nonexclusive or" is intended, the condition will specify "or both" as, for example, in *The committee must include Saito or Williams or both.* When abbreviating conditions of these kinds, you may find it best to use two-part representations such as:

"Exclusive or"	S|W but ^(SW)
"Nonexclusive or"	S|W or (SW)

Alternatively, you could use separate symbols for "exclusive or" and "nonexclusive or." For example, if you use a vertical line to represent "nonexclusive or," you could use a pair of vertical lines to represent "exclusive or," like this:

"Exclusive or"	X||Y
"Nonexclusive or"	X|Y

Diagramming the Setup and Conditions
Now that you've looked at some ways to represent conditions, let's look at a couple of examples of how to diagram a complete Analytical Reasoning passage.

Here's an Analytical Reasoning passage involving ordering relationships:

On one afternoon, an accountant will meet individually with each of exactly five clients—Reilly, Sanchez, Tang, Upton, and Yansky—and will also go to the gym alone for a workout. The accountant's workout and five meetings will each start at either 1:00, 2:00, 3:00, 4:00, 5:00, or 6:00. The following conditions must apply:
  The meeting with Sanchez is earlier than the workout.
  The workout is earlier than the meeting with Tang.
  The meeting with Yansky is either immediately before or immediately after the workout.
  The meeting with Upton is earlier than the meeting with Reilly.

In this case, the task is to determine a schedule for the accountant's five meetings and workout. These six appointments can be abbreviated by their initials: R, S, T, U, Y, and W. The setup tells you that each of these appointments will start at 1:00, 2:00, 3:00, 4:00, 5:00, or 6:00, with the six appointments each beginning at a different one of these six times. So, along with a list of initials for the six appointments, you can begin with a simple diagram of the schedule like the following, with slots for each of the six times:

The appointments: R S T U Y W

The schedule:

—	—	—	—	—	—
1	2	3	4	5	6

Now let's abbreviate the conditions that constrain the schedule for the six appointments. The first condition (*The meeting with Sanchez is earlier than the workout.*) can be abbreviated:

S..W

The second condition (*The workout is earlier than the meeting with Tang.*) can be abbreviated:

W..T

Notice that these two conditions can be condensed into a single representation:

S..W..T

The third condition (*The meeting with Yansky is either immediately before or immediately after the workout.*) can be abbreviated like this:

Y⌣W

Here, the squiggle indicates that the relative order of the meeting with Yansky and the workout is not fixed but there is nothing that comes between the two.

This condition can be folded in with what we've got so far, like this:

S..Y∫W..T

The fourth condition (*The meeting with Upton is earlier than the meeting with Reilly.*) can be abbreviated like this:

U..R

This last condition cannot be combined with anything else we've derived so far, so you're done with representing the conditions.

So the entire passage now boils down to this:

The appointments: R   S   T   U   Y   W

The schedule:

$\overline{1}$ $\overline{2}$ $\overline{3}$ $\overline{4}$ $\overline{5}$ $\overline{6}$

The conditions: S..Y∫W..T

                       U..R

Notice that in this case all of the six elements—the meeting with Reilly (R), the meeting with Sanchez (S), the meeting with Tang (T), the meeting with Upton (U), the meeting with Yansky (Y), and the workout (W)—are mentioned in the conditions. So in this case there's really no danger of forgetting to keep track of all the elements. Be careful when working through other sets of Analytical Reasoning questions, though, being sure not to forget about any of the elements that are presented in the setup but that aren't explicitly mentioned in the conditions.

Looking at the abbreviated conditions for this example passage, you can already make several inferences, such as these:

- The only elements that can be last are Tang and Reilly.

- The only elements that can be first are Sanchez and Upton.

Inferences such as these can be very helpful when it comes time to answer the questions.

Now let's look at another example, this one involving grouping relationships:

A town is planning to plant trees in its two public parks—Graystone Park and Landing Park. There are exactly four varieties of trees available—hickories, maples, oaks, and sycamores. Each of the parks will have exactly three of the varieties. The selection of varieties for the parks conforms to the following conditions:
   At least one of the parks must have both maples and sycamores.
   Any park that has oaks must also have hickories.
   Graystone Park must have maples.

In this case, the task is to select types of trees for the two parks.

Reading the setup, you see that there are two parks, and that each park will have exactly three types of trees. Abbreviating the names of the parks to G and L, you can represent the structure of the possible outcomes like this:

G   L

_   _

_   _

_   _

or like this:

G: _ _ _

L: _ _ _

Next, you can abbreviate the types of trees as H, M, O, and S. Notice that so far we don't know whether all of the types of trees must be selected or whether it's acceptable to distribute only a subset of them between the two parks. Unless you find something to the contrary when you examine the conditions, you should assume that it's possible that fewer than all four of the types of trees can appear in a possible outcome.

Now abbreviate the conditions. The first condition (*At least one of the parks must have both maples and sycamores.*) might be abbreviated something like this:

≥ 1P(MS)

or maybe something like this:

1+ P: M&S

Here, "≥ 1P" or "1+ P" is used to represent at least one of the parks, and "(MS)" or "M&S" is used to represent *both maples and sycamores*.

The second condition is *Any park that has oaks must also have hickories*. This is equivalent to *If a park has oaks, then it must also have hickories*. So this condition can be represented like any other conditional statement and can be abbreviated like this:

O → H

The third condition (*Graystone Park must have maples.*) can be abbreviated in either of the following ways:

G:M G_M

Remember, it doesn't matter what form your abbreviations take, as long as they are meaningful to you. The only thing you need to do is pick a set of abbreviations and use them consistently.

Now notice that you can fold that last condition into your representation of the structure of the possible outcomes, like this:

G: M _ _

L: _ _ _

So here's one complete representation of what you have for this setup and conditions:

G: M _ _   H M O S   1+P: M&S

L: _ _ _   O → H

What this tells you is this:

- There will be three types of trees selected for each of the two parks, and one of the types selected for Graystone will be maples.

- There are four types of trees to select from: hickories, maples, oaks, and sycamores.

- At least one of the parks must have both maples and sycamores.

- Any park that has oaks must also have hickories.

Note that there are some inferences you can make from this, including these:

- If Graystone doesn't have sycamores, then Landing must have both maples and sycamores. Otherwise, there won't be at least one park that has both maples and sycamores.

- If a park has both maples and sycamores, that park can't also have oaks. This is because each park has exactly three types of trees, but if there are oaks there must also be hickories, which would mean that if there are oaks along with maples and sycamores, you'd need to have all four types of trees, rather than exactly three.

These sorts of inferences could come in handy when it comes time to answer the questions.

Now let's look at an example that involves both ordering and grouping:

During a music concert, exactly five solo pieces—Grace, Honor, Joy, Kite, Lilacs—will be performed one after the other. Each piece will be performed once and will be performed either on the flute, the piano, or the violin, subject to the following constraints:
Both Grace and Honor must be performed earlier than Lilacs.
Both Grace and Joy must be performed on the flute.
The second piece must be performed on the violin.
The third piece performed must be Kite.

In this case, we have two sets of things: the solo pieces and the instruments on which the pieces will be performed. So you need two sets of abbreviations, one for the solos and one for the instruments:

G H J K L

F P V

If you want, you can label each of these groups. For example, you could label the first of them S (for "solo") and the second of them I (for "instrument"), like this:

S: G H J K L

I: F P V

The setup tells you that the pieces are to be performed one at a time, once each. So the basic structure of the possible outcomes can be represented something like this:

```
  1     2     3     4     5
  ─     ─     ─     ─     ─
```

This isn't quite complete yet, though. You also need to keep track of which instrument each of the solos is performed on. A good way to do that is to have another set of dashes below the first set, like this:

```
  1     2     3     4     5
  ─     ─     ─     ─     ─
  ─     ─     ─     ─     ─
```

Here, the first line of dashes is for the solos and the second line of dashes is for the instruments on which the corresponding solos are played. You can make this explicit by labeling the lines, if you like:

```
        1     2     3     4     5
   S:    ─     ─     ─     ─     ─
   I:    ─     ─     ─     ─     ─
```

Now let's abbreviate the conditions. The first condition (*Both Grace and Honor must be performed earlier than Lilacs.*) can be abbreviated like this:

G|H..H|G..L

This means that in an acceptable outcome, *Grace, Honor, and Lilacs* will be ordered so that either *Grace* is performed at some time earlier than *Honor* and then *Lilacs* is performed at some time later than *Honor*, or *Honor* is performed at some time earlier than *Grace* and then *Lilacs* is performed at some time later than *Grace*.

The second condition (*Both Grace and Joy must be performed on the flute.*) can be abbreviated like this:

G_F J_F

The third condition (*The second piece must be performed on the violin.*) can be abbreviated like this:

V_2

Notice that the third condition can be folded into the representation of the basic structure of possible outcomes like this:

```
        1     2     3     4     5
   S:    ─     ─     ─     ─     ─
   I:    ─     V     ─     ─     ─
```

The fourth condition (*The third piece performed must be Kite.*) can be abbreviated like this:

K_3

Notice that this, too, can be folded into the representation of the basic structure:

```
        1     2     3     4     5
   S:    ─     ─     K     ─     ─
   I:    ─     V     ─     ─     ─
```

So here is a complete representation of the information given in the setup and conditions:

```
        1     2     3     4     5
   S:    ─     ─     K     ─     ─
   I:    ─     V     ─     ─     ─

   S: G  H  J  K  L          G|H..H|G..L
   I: F  P  V                $G_F$      $J_F$
```

Notice that you can draw several inferences from this, including these:

• Neither *Grace* nor *Joy* can be performed second (since the second performance must be performed on the violin, but *Grace* and *Joy* must both be performed on the flute).

• The only solos that can be performed fifth are *Joy* and *Lilacs*.

• The earliest that *Lilacs* can be performed is fourth.

These sorts of inferences can be helpful when it comes to answering the questions.

Diagramming the Questions

Once you have a diagram for the passage, you might find that that's all you'll need to answer some or all of the questions that are based on that passage. Sometimes, though, you'll want to have separate, additional diagrams for particular questions.

Consider again the ordering passage we looked at in the previous section:

> On one afternoon, an accountant will meet individually with each of exactly five clients—Reilly, Sanchez, Tang, Upton, and Yansky—and will also go to the gym alone for a workout. The accountant's workout and five meetings will each start at either 1:00, 2:00, 3:00, 4:00, 5:00, or 6:00. The following conditions must apply:
> The meeting with Sanchez is earlier than the workout.
> The workout is earlier than the meeting with Tang.
> The meeting with Yansky is either immediately before or immediately after the workout.
> The meeting with Upton is earlier than the meeting with Reilly.

We found that the setup and conditions for this passage could be represented in abbreviated form like this:

The appointments: R S T U Y W

The schedule:

$$\overline{1} \quad \overline{2} \quad \overline{3} \quad \overline{4} \quad \overline{5} \quad \overline{6}$$

The conditions: S..Y∫W..T
                    U..R

Now suppose that for this passage you have a question like this:

If the meeting with Tang is at 4:00, which one of the following must be true?

(A) The meeting with Reilly is at 5:00.
(B) The meeting with Upton is at 5:00.
(C) The meeting with Yansky is at 2:00.
(D) The meeting with Yansky is at 3:00.
(E) The workout is at 2:00.

After sketching out a new version of the basic structure of the outcome, you can insert T in the fourth position, to indicate Tang at 4:00:

$$\overline{1} \quad \overline{2} \quad \overline{3} \quad \overset{T}{\overline{4}} \quad \overline{5} \quad \overline{6}$$

Then, after examining the first of your abbreviated conditions, you can see that the only possibilities for Sanchez, Yansky, and the workout are for Sanchez to be first, and for either Yansky or the workout to be second, and for either the workout or Yansky to be third, which you can represent like this:

$$\overset{S}{\overline{1}} \quad \overset{Y|W}{\overline{2}} \quad \overset{W|Y}{\overline{3}} \quad \overset{T}{\overline{4}} \quad \overline{5} \quad \overline{6}$$

Looking at the other abbreviated conditions, you see that the only possibilities for Upton and Reilly are for Upton to be fifth and for Reilly to be sixth:

$$\overset{S}{\overline{1}} \quad \overset{Y|W}{\overline{2}} \quad \overset{W|Y}{\overline{3}} \quad \overset{T}{\overline{4}} \quad \overset{U}{\overline{5}} \quad \overset{R}{\overline{6}}$$

Looking at this diagram, you can rule out all of the answer choices except (B): *The meeting with Upton is at 5:00.*[†] So the correct answer here is (B).

Now let's consider the grouping passage we looked at in the previous section:

> A town is planning to plant trees in its two public parks—Graystone Park and Landing Park. There are exactly four varieties of trees available—hickories, maples, oaks, and sycamores. Each of the parks will have exactly three of the varieties. The selection of varieties for the parks conforms to the following conditions:
> At least one of the parks must have both maples and sycamores.
> Any park that has oaks must also have hickories.
> Graystone Park must have maples.

We found that the setup and conditions for this passage could be represented like this:

G: M _ _   H M O S   1+ P: M&S

L: _ _ _   O →H

[†] Since Reilly's meeting can't be at 5:00, you can rule out (A). Since Yansky's meeting can be at either 2:00 or 3:00, you can rule out (C) and (D). And since the workout can be at either 2:00 or 3:00, you can rule out (E).

Now suppose that for this passage you have a question like this:

Which one of the following CANNOT be true?

(A) *Both parks have oaks.*
(B) *Both parks have hickories.*
(C) *Both parks have sycamores.*
(D) *Exactly one of the parks has maples.*
(E) *Exactly one of the parks has sycamores.*

You may recall from the discussion of the setup and conditions that it's impossible to have oaks in both of the parks. This is because each of the parks has exactly three types of trees, at least one of the parks must have both maples and sycamores, and any park that has oaks must also have hickories. Whether Graystone has maples and sycamores or Landing has maples and sycamores, or both Graystone and Landing have maples and sycamores, it wouldn't be possible to have oaks in both of the parks:

G: M̲ S̲ O̲   (no room for hickories)
L: O̲ _ _

G: M̲ O̲ _
L: M̲ S̲ O̲ (no room for hickories)

G: M̲ S̲ O̲ (no room for hickories)
L: M̲ S̲ O̲ (no room for hickories)

If you try to select oaks along with maples and sycamores, you'll also have to select hickories; but this would give you four types of trees selected for a single park, which is unacceptable. Therefore, (A) cannot be true and so is the correct answer here.

Next, let's consider again the example passage that involves both ordering and grouping:

During a music concert, exactly five solo pieces—Grace, Honor, Joy, Kite, Lilacs—will be performed one after the other. Each piece will be performed once and will be performed either on the flute, the piano, or the violin, subject to the following constraints:
  Both Grace and Honor must be performed earlier than Lilacs.
  Both Grace and Joy must be performed on the flute.
  The second piece must be performed on the violin.
  The third piece performed must be Kite.

As you saw earlier, the information in the setup and conditions can be represented like this:

	1	2	3	4	5
S:	–	–	K̲	–	–
I:	–	V̲	–	–	–

S: G H J K L   G|H..H|G..L
I: F P V   G_F   J_F

Now suppose that for this passage you have a question like this:

If Joy is performed earlier than Grace, which one of the following must be true?

(A) *The third piece is performed on the flute.*
(B) *The fourth piece is performed on the flute.*
(C) *The fourth piece is performed on the violin.*
(D) *The fifth piece is performed on the flute.*
(E) *The fifth piece is performed on the violin.*

You know from the second of our abbreviated conditions that neither *Joy* nor *Grace*, both of which must be performed on the flute, can be performed second, since the second solo must be performed on the violin. From the first of our abbreviated conditions, you know that *Lilacs* also can't be performed second, since Lilacs has to be performed later than both *Grace* and *Honor*. Since *Kite* must be performed third, that leaves only *Honor* available for the second solo:

	1	2	3	4	5
S:	–	H̲	K̲	–	–
I:	–	V̲	–	–	–

Since *Lilacs* has to be performed later than *Grace*, and since, according to the new supposition for this question, *Joy* must be performed earlier than *Grace*, the order for all of the solos is now fixed:

	1	2	3	4	5
S:	J̲	H̲	K̲	G̲	L̲
I:	–	V̲	–	–	–

Finally, since you know that *Joy* and *Grace* must both be performed on the flute, you can further fill in your diagram like this:

	1	2	3	4	5
S:	J	H	K	G	L
I:	F	V	—	F	—

Nothing restricts which instruments are used for the third and fifth solos, so at this point you can see that (B), *The fourth piece is performed on the flute*, must be true (and although some of the other answer choices *can* be true, none of them *must* be true). So (B) is the correct answer.

Concluding Remarks

The examples presented in this discussion should give you some good ideas for how to use abbreviations and diagrams to help in answering Analytical Reasoning questions. These examples are far from exhaustive, however, so don't assume that all Analytical Reasoning questions will look exactly like these. Above all, remember that your goal should be to find a system for representing Analytical Reasoning setups and conditions that *you* are comfortable with.

APPENDIX B: LOGICAL REASONING QUESTIONS

The Volunteers for Literacy Program would benefit if Dolores takes Victor's place as director, since Dolores is far more skillful than Victor is at securing the kind of financial support the program needs and Dolores does not have Victor's propensity for alienating the program's most dedicated volunteers.

The pattern of reasoning in the argument above is most closely paralleled in which one of the following?

*(A) It would be more convenient for Dominique to take a bus to school than to take the subway, since the bus stops closer to her house than does the subway and, unlike the subway, the bus goes directly to the school.

(B) Joshua's interest would be better served by taking the bus to get to his parent's house rather than by taking an airplane, since his primary concern is to travel as cheaply as possible and taking the bus is less expensive than going by airplane.

(C) Belinda will get to the concert more quickly by subway than by taxi, since the concert takes place on a Friday evening and on Friday evenings traffic near the concert hall is exceptionally heavy.

(D) Anita would benefit financially by taking the train to work rather than driving her car, since when she drives she has to pay parking fees and the daily fee for parking a car is higher than a round-trip train ticket.

(E) It would be to Fred's advantage to exchange his bus tickets for train tickets, since he needs to arrive at his meeting before any of the other participants and if he goes by bus at least one of the other participants will arrive first.

The years 1917, 1937, 1956, 1968, 1979, and 1990 are all notable for the occurrence of both popular uprisings and near-maximum sunspot activity. During heavy sunspot activity, there is a sharp rise in positively charged ions in the air people breathe, and positively charged ions are known to make people anxious and irritable. Therefore, it is likely that sunspot activity has actually been a factor in triggering popular uprisings.

Which one of the following exhibits a pattern of reasoning most similar to that in the passage?

(A) The ancient Greeks sometimes attempted to predict the outcome of future events by watching the flight patterns of birds. Since the events themselves often matched the predictions, the birds were probably responding to some factor that also influenced the events.

(B) Martha, Sidney, and Hilary are the city's three most powerful politicians, and all three graduated from Ridgeview High School. Although Ridgeview never had a reputation for excellence, it must have been a good school to have produced three such successful graduates.

(C) Unusually cold weather last December coincided with a rise in fuel prices. When it is cold, people use more fuel to keep warm; and when more fuel is used, prices rise. Therefore if prices are high next winter, it will be the result of cold weather.

(D) The thirty healthiest people in a long-term medical study turned out to be the same thirty whose regular diets included the most vegetables. Since specific substances in vegetables are known to help the body fight disease, vegetables should be part of everyone's diet.

*(E) Acme's most productive managers are consistently those who occupy the corner offices, which have more windows than other offices at Acme. Since people are more alert when they are exposed to abundant natural light, the greater productivity of these managers is probably at least in part a result of their working in the corner offices.

Lydia: Red squirrels are known to make holes in the bark of sugar maple trees and to consume the trees' sap. Since sugar maple sap is essentially water with a small concentration of sugar, the squirrels almost certainly are after either water or sugar. Water is easily available from other sources in places where maple trees grow, so the squirrels would not go to the trouble of chewing holes in trees just to get water. Therefore, they are probably after the sugar.

Galina: It must be something other than sugar, because the concentration of sugar in the maple sap is so low that a squirrel would need to drink an enormous amount of sap to get any significant amount of sugar.

Lydia's argument proceeds by

(A)   dismissing potentially disconfirming data
(B)   citing a general rule of which the conclusion is a specific instance
(C)   presenting an observed action as part of a larger pattern of behavior
(D)   drawing an analogy between well-understood phenomena and an unexplained phenomenon
*(E)   rejecting a possible alternative explanation for an observed phenomenon

In order to determine automobile insurance premiums for a driver, insurance companies calculate various risk factors; as the risk factors increase, so does the premium. Certain factors, such as the driver's age and past accident history, play an important role in these calculations. Yet these premiums should also increase with the frequency with which a person drives. After all, a person's chance of being involved in a mishap increases in proportion to the number of times that person drives.

The claim that insurance premiums should increase as the frequency with which a driver drives increases plays which one of the following roles in the argument?

(A)   a premise of the argument
*(B)   the conclusion of the argument
(C)   evidence offered in support of one of the premises
(D)   an assertion phrased to preclude an anticipated objection
(E)   a clarification of a key term in the argument

Zachary: The term "fresco" refers to paint that has been applied to wet plaster. Once dried, a fresco indelibly preserves the paint that a painter has applied in this way. Unfortunately, additions known to have been made by later painters have obscured the original fresco work done by Michelangelo in the Sistine Chapel. Therefore, in order to restore Michelangelo's Sistine Chapel paintings to the appearance that Michelangelo intended them to have, everything except the original fresco work must be stripped away.

Stephen: But it was extremely common for painters of Michelangelo's era to add painted details to their own fresco work after the frescoes had dried.

Stephen's response to Zachary proceeds by

*(A)   calling into question an assumption on which Zachary's conclusion depends
(B)   challenging the definition of a key term in Zachary's argument
(C)   drawing a conclusion other than the one that Zachary reaches
(D)   denying the truth of one of the stated premises of Zachary's argument
(E)   demonstrating that Zachary's conclusion is not consistent with the premises he uses to support it

Journalist: Obviously, though some animals are purely carnivorous, none would survive without plants. But the dependence is mutual. Many plant species would never have come to be had there been no animals to pollinate, fertilize, and broadcast their seeds. Also, plants' photosynthetic activity would deplete the carbon dioxide in Earth's atmosphere were it not constantly being replenished by the exhalation of animals, engine fumes, and smoke from fires, many set by human beings.

Which one of the following most accurately expresses the main conclusion of the journalist's argument?

(A)   The photosynthetic activity of plants is necessary for animal life, but animal life is also necessary for the occurrence of photosynthesis in plants.
(B)   Some purely carnivorous animals would not survive without plants.
(C)   The chemical composition of Earth and its atmosphere depends, at least to some extent, on the existence and activities of the animals that populate Earth.
(D)   Human activity is part of what prevents plants from depleting the oxygen in Earth's atmosphere on which plants and animals alike depend.
*(E)   Just as animals are dependent on plants for their survival, plants are dependent on animals for theirs.

All known deposits of the mineral tanzanite are in Tanzania. Therefore, because Ashley collects only tanzanite stones, she is unlikely ever to collect a stone not originally from Tanzania.

Which one of the following is most similar in its reasoning to the argument above?

(A)   The lagoon on Scrag Island is home to many frogs. Since the owls on Scrag Island eat nothing but frogs from the island, the owls will probably never eat many frogs that live outside the lagoon.
(B)   Every frog ever seen on Scrag Island lives in the lagoon. The frogs on the island are eaten only by the owls on the island, and hence the owls may never eat an animal that lives outside the lagoon.
(C)   Frogs are the only animals known to live in the lagoon on Scrag Island. The diet of the owls on Scrag Island consists of nothing but frogs from the island. Therefore, the owls are unlikely ever to eat an animal that lives outside the lagoon.
*(D) The only frogs yet discovered on Scrag Island live in the lagoon. The diet of all the owls on Scrag Island consists entirely of frogs on the island, so the owls will probably never eat an animal that lives outside the lagoon.
(E)   Each frog on Scrag Island lives in the lagoon. No owl on Scrag Island is known to eat anything but frogs on the island. It follows that no owl on Scrag Island will eat anything that lives outside the lagoon.

Any sale item that is purchased can be returned for store credit but not for a refund of the purchase price. Every home appliance and every piece of gardening equipment is on sale along with selected construction tools.

If the statements above are true, which one of the following must also be true?

(A)   Any item that is not a home appliance or a piece of gardening equipment is returnable for a refund.
(B)   Any item that is not on sale cannot be returned for store credit.
(C)   Some construction tools are not returnable for store credit.
*(D) No piece of gardening equipment is returnable for a refund.
(E)   None of the things that are returnable for a refund are construction tools.

People should avoid taking the antacid calcium carbonate in doses larger than half a gram, for despite its capacity to neutralize stomach acids, calcium carbonate can increase the calcium level in the blood and thus impair kidney function. Moreover, just half a gram of it can stimulate the production of gastrin, a stomach hormone that triggers acid secretion.

Which one of the following is most strongly supported by the information above?

(A)   Cessation of gastrin production is a more effective method of controlling excess stomach acid than is direct neutralization of stomach acid.
(B)   People who avoid taking more than half a gram of calcium carbonate are less likely than average to suffer from impaired kidney function.
(C)   Doses of calcium carbonate smaller than half a gram can reduce stomach acid more effectively than much larger doses do.
*(D) Half a gram of calcium carbonate can causally contribute to both the secretion and the neutralization of stomach acids.
(E)   Impaired kidney function may increase the level of calcium in the blood.

Mary: Computers will make more information available to ordinary people than was ever available before, thus making it easier for them to acquire knowledge without consulting experts.
Joyce: As more knowledge became available in previous centuries, the need for specialists to synthesize and explain it to nonspecialists increased. So computers will probably create a greater dependency on experts.

The dialogue most strongly supports the claim that Mary and Joyce disagree with each other about whether

(A)   computers will contribute only negligibly to the increasing dissemination of knowledge in society
*(B) computers will increase the need for ordinary people seeking knowledge to turn to experts
(C)   computers will make more information available to ordinary people
(D)   dependency on computers will increase with the increase of knowledge
(E)   synthesizing knowledge and explaining it to ordinary people can be accomplished only by computer experts

Toxicologist: A survey of oil-refinery workers who work with MBTE, an ingredient currently used in some smog-reducing gasolines, found an alarming incidence of complaints about headaches, fatigue, and shortness of breath. Since gasoline containing MBTE will soon be widely used, we can expect an increased incidence of headaches, fatigue, and shortness of breath.

Each of the following, if true, strengthens the toxicologist's argument EXCEPT:

(A)   Most oil-refinery workers who do not work with MBTE do not have serious health problems involving headaches, fatigue, and shortness of breath.
*(B)   Headaches, fatigue, and shortness of breath are among the symptoms of several medical conditions that are potentially serious threats to public health.
(C)   Since the time when gasoline containing MBTE was first introduced in a few metropolitan areas, those areas reported an increase in the number of complaints about headaches, fatigue, and shortness of breath.
(D)   Regions in which only gasoline containing MBTE is used have a much greater incidence of headaches, fatigue, and shortness of breath than do similar regions in which only MBTE-free gasoline is used.
(E)   The oil-refinery workers surveyed were carefully selected to be representative of the broader population in their medical histories prior to exposure to MBTE, as well as in other relevant respects.

A recent study reveals that television advertising does not significantly affect children's preferences for breakfast cereals. The study compared two groups of children. One group had watched no television, and the other group had watched average amounts of television and its advertising. Both groups strongly preferred the sugary cereals heavily advertised on television.

Which one of the following statements, if true, most weakens the argument?

*(A)   The preferences of children who do not watch television advertising are influenced by the preferences of children who watch the advertising.
(B)   The preference for sweets is not a universal trait in humans, and can be influenced by environmental factors such as television advertising.
(C)   Most of the children in the group that had watched television were already familiar with the advertisements for these cereals.
(D)   Both groups rejected cereals low in sugar even when these cereals were heavily advertised on television.
(E)   Cereal preferences of adults who watch television are known to be significantly different from the cereal preferences of adults who do not watch television.

Vague laws set vague limits on people's freedom, which makes it impossible for them to know for certain whether their actions are legal. Thus, under vague laws people cannot feel secure.

The conclusion follows logically if which one of the following is assumed?

*(A)   People can feel secure only if they know for certain whether their actions are legal.
(B)   If people do not know for certain whether their actions are legal, then they might not feel secure.
(C)   If people know for certain whether their actions are legal, they can feel secure.
(D)   People can feel secure if they are governed by laws that are not vague.
(E)   Only people who feel secure can know for certain whether their actions are legal.

Since Mayor Drabble always repays her political debts as soon as possible, she will almost certainly appoint Lee to be the new head of the arts commission. Lee has wanted that job for a long time, and Drabble owes Lee a lot for his support in the last election.

Which one of the following is an assumption on which the argument depends?

*(A) Mayor Drabble has no political debt that is both of longer standing than the one she owes to Lee and could as suitably be repaid by an appointment to be the new head of the arts commission.
(B) There is no one to whom Mayor Drabble owes a greater political debt for support in the last election than the political debt she owes to Lee.
(C) Lee is the only person to whom Mayor Drabble owes a political debt who would be willing to accept an appointment from her as the new head of the arts commission.
(D) Whether Lee is qualified to head the arts commission is irrelevant to Mayor Drabble's decision.
(E) The only way that Mayor Drabble can adequately repay her political debt to Lee is by appointing him to head the arts commission.

Advertisement: Attention pond owners! Ninety-eight percent of mosquito larvae in a pond die within minutes after the pond has been treated with BTI. Yet BTI is not toxic to fish, birds, animals, plants, or beneficial insects. So by using BTI regularly to destroy their larvae, you can greatly reduce populations of pesky mosquitoes that hatch in your pond, and you can do so without diminishing the populations of fish, frogs, or beneficial insects in and around the pond.

Which one of the following is an assumption on which the argument depends?

(A) The most effective way to control the numbers of mosquitoes in a given area is to destroy the mosquito larvae in that area.
(B) Populations of mosquitoes are not dependent on a single body of water within an area as a place for their larvae to hatch and develop.
(C) There are no insect pests besides mosquitoes that pond owners might want to eliminate from in and around their ponds.
(D) The effectiveness of BTI in destroying mosquito larvae in a pond does not require the pond owner's strict adherence to specific application procedures.

*(E) The fish, frogs, and beneficial insects in and around a pond-owner's pond do not depend on mosquito larvae as an important source of food.

People who receive unsolicited advice from someone whose advantage would be served if that advice is taken should regard the proffered advice with skepticism unless there is good reason to think that their interests substantially coincide with those of the advice giver in the circumstance in question.

This principle, if accepted, would justify which one of the following judgments?

(A) After learning by chance that Harriet is looking for a secure investment for her retirement savings, Floyd writes to her recommending the R&M Company as an especially secure investment. But since Floyd is the sole owner of R&M, Harriet should reject his advice out of hand and invest her savings elsewhere.
*(B) While shopping for a refrigerator, Ramón is approached by a salesperson who, on the basis of her personal experience, warns him against the least expensive model. However, the salesperson's commission increases with the price of the refrigerator sold, so Ramón should not reject the least expensive model on the salesperson's advice alone.
(C) Mario wants to bring pastry to Yvette's party, and when he consults her Yvette suggests that he bring his favorite chocolate fudge brownies from the local bakery. However, since Yvette also prefers those brownies to any other pastry, Mario would be wise to check with others before following her recommendation.
(D) Sara overhears Ron talking about a course he will be teaching and interrupts to recommend a textbook for his course. However, even though Sara and Ron each wrote a chapter of this textbook, since the book's editor is a personal friend of Sara's, Ron should investigate further before deciding whether it is the best textbook for his course.
(E) Mei is buying fish for soup. Joel, who owns the fish market where Mei is a regular and valued customer, suggests a much less expensive fish than the fish Mei herself prefers. Since if Mei follows Joel's advice, Joel will make less profit on the sale than he would have otherwise, Mei should follow his recommendation.

Marianne is a professional chess player who hums audibly while playing her matches, thereby distracting her opponents. When ordered by chess officials to cease humming or else be disqualified from professional chess, Marianne protested the order. She argued that since she was unaware of her humming, her humming was involuntary and that therefore she should not be held responsible for it.

Which one of the following principles, if valid, most helps to support Marianne's argument against the order?

(A) Chess players who hum audibly while playing their matches should not protest if their opponents also hum.
*(B) Of a player's actions, only those that are voluntary should be used as justification for disqualifying that player from professional chess.
(C) A person should be held responsible for those involuntary actions that serve that person's interests.
(D) Types of behavior that are not considered voluntary in everyday circumstances should be considered voluntary if they occur in the context of a professional chess match.
(E) Chess players should be disqualified from professional chess matches if they regularly attempt to distract their opponents.

Physicist: The claim that low-temperature nuclear fusion can be achieved entirely by chemical means is based on chemical experiments in which the measurements and calculations are inaccurate.

Chemist: But your challenge is ineffectual, since you are simply jealous at the thought that chemists might have solved a problem that physicists have been unable to solve.

Which one of the following is the strongest criticism of the chemist's response to the physicist's challenge?

(A) It restates a claim in different words instead of offering evidence for this claim.
(B) It fails to establish that perfect accuracy of measurements and calculations is possible.
(C) It confuses two different meanings of the word "solve."
*(D) It is directed against the proponent of a claim rather than against the claim itself.
(E) It rests on a contradiction.

Morris High School has introduced a policy designed to improve the working conditions of its new teachers. As a result of this policy, only one-quarter of all part-time teachers now quit during their first year. However, a third of all full-time teachers now quit during their first year. Thus, more full-time than part-time teachers at Morris now quit during their first year.

The argument's reasoning is questionable because the argument fails to rule out the possibility that

(A) before the new policy was instituted, more part-time than full-time teachers at Morris High School used to quit during their first year
(B) before the new policy was instituted, the same number of full-time teachers as part-time teachers at Morris High School used to quit during their first year
(C) Morris High School employs more new full-time teachers than new part-time teachers
*(D) Morris High School employs more new part-time teachers than new full-time teachers
(E) Morris High School employs the same number of new part-time as new full-time teachers

If Blankenship Enterprises has to switch suppliers in the middle of a large production run, the company will not show a profit for the year. Therefore, if Blankenship Enterprises in fact turns out to show no profit for the year, it will also turn out to be true that the company had to switch suppliers during a large production run.

The reasoning in the argument is most vulnerable to criticism on which one of the following grounds?

(A) The argument is a circular argument made up of an opening claim followed by a conclusion that merely paraphrases that claim.
*(B) The argument fails to establish that a condition under which a phenomenon is said to occur is the only condition under which that phenomenon occurs.
(C) The argument involves an equivocation, in that the word "profit" is allowed to shift its meaning during the course of the argument.
(D) The argument erroneously uses an exceptional, isolated case to support a universal conclusion.
(E) The argument explains one event as being caused by another event, even though both events must actually have been caused by some third, unidentified event.

If the majority of the residents of the apartment complex complain that their apartments are infested with ants, then the management of the complex will have to engage the services of an exterminator. But the majority of the residents of the complex indicate that their apartments are virtually free of ants. Therefore, the management of the complex will not have to engage the services of an exterminator.

Which one of the following arguments contains a flawed pattern of reasoning parallel to that contained in the argument above?

(A)   A theater will be constructed in the fall if funds collected are at least sufficient to cover its cost. To date, the funds collected exceed the theater's cost, so the theater will be constructed in the fall.
(B)   The number of flights operated by the airlines cannot be reduced unless the airlines can collect higher airfares. But people will not pay higher airfares, so it is not the case that the number of flights will be reduced.
(C)   In order for the company to start the proposed building project, both the town council and the mayor must approve. Since the mayor has already approved, the building project will be started soon.
*(D) Most employees will attend the company picnic if the entertainment committee is successful in getting a certain band to play at the picnic. But that band will be out of the country on the day of the picnic, so it is not true that most employees will attend.
(E)   Either the school's principal or two-thirds of the parent council must approve a change in the school dress code in order for the code to be changed. Since the principal will not approve a change in the dress code, the code will not be changed.

The company that produces XYZ, a computer spreadsheet program, estimates that millions of illegally reproduced copies of XYZ are being used. If legally purchased, this number of copies would have generated millions of dollars in sales for the company, yet despite a company-wide effort to boost sales, the company has not taken available legal measures to prosecute those who have copied the program illegally.

Which one of the following, if true, most helps to explain why the company has not taken available legal measures?

(A)   XYZ is very difficult to copy illegally, because a sophisticated anticopying mechanism in the program must first be disabled.
(B)   The legal measures that the company that produces XYZ could take against those who have copied its product became available several years before XYZ came on the market.
*(C) Many people who purchase a software program like XYZ are willing to purchase that program only after they have already used it.
(D)   The number of illegally reproduced copies of XYZ currently in use exceeds the number of legally reproduced copies currently in use.
(E)   The company that produces ABC, the spreadsheet program that is XYZ's main rival in the marketplace, is well known for taking legal action against people who have copied ABC illegally.

Of the five bill collectors at Apex Collection Agency, Mr. Young has the highest rate of unsuccessful collections. Yet Mr. Young is the best bill collector on the agency's staff.

Which one of the following, if true, most helps to resolve the apparent discrepancy?

*(A) Mr. Young is assigned the majority of the most difficult cases at the agency.
(B)   The other four bill collectors at the agency all consider Mr. Young to be a very capable bill collector.
(C)   Mr. Young's rate of collections per year has remained fairly steady in the last few years.
(D)   Before joining the agency, Mr. Young was affiliated with the credit department of a large department store.
(E)   None of the bill collectors at the agency has been on the agency's staff longer than Mr. Young has.

Some philosophers find the traditional, subjective approach to studying the mind outdated and ineffectual. For them, the attempt to describe the sensation of pain or anger, for example, or the

(5) awareness that one is aware, has been surpassed by advances in fields such as psychology, neuroscience, and cognitive science. Scientists, they claim, do not concern themselves with how a phenomenon feels from the inside; instead of investigating private evidence

(10) perceivable only to a particular individual, scientists pursue hard data—such as the study of how nerves transmit impulses to the brain—which is externally observable and can be described without reference to any particular point of view. With respect to features of

(15) the universe such as those investigated by chemistry, biology, and physics, this objective approach has been remarkably successful in yielding knowledge. Why, these philosophers ask, should we suppose the mind to be any different?

(20) But philosophers loyal to subjectivity are not persuaded by appeals to science when such appeals conflict with the data gathered by introspection. Knowledge, they argue, relies on the data of experience, which includes subjective experience. Why

(25) should philosophy ally itself with scientists who would reduce the sources of knowledge to only those data that can be discerned objectively?

On the face of it, it seems unlikely that these two approaches to studying the mind could be reconciled.

(30) Because philosophy, unlike science, does not progress inexorably toward a single truth, disputes concerning the nature of the mind are bound to continue. But what is particularly distressing about the present debate is that genuine communication between the two sides is

(35) virtually impossible. For reasoned discourse to occur, there must be shared assumptions or beliefs. Starting from radically divergent perspectives, subjectivists and objectivists lack a common context in which to consider evidence presented from each other's

(40) perspectives.

The situation may be likened to a debate between adherents of different religions about the creation of the universe. While each religion may be confident that its cosmology is firmly grounded in its respective

(45) sacred text, there is little hope that conflicts between their competing cosmologies could be resolved by recourse to the texts alone. Only further investigation into the authority of the texts themselves would be sufficient.

(50) What would be required to resolve the debate between the philosophers of mind, then, is an investigation into the authority of their differing perspectives. How rational is it to take scientific description as the ideal way to understand the nature of

(55) consciousness? Conversely, how useful is it to rely solely on introspection for one's knowledge about the workings of the mind? Are there alternative ways of gaining such knowledge? In this debate, epistemology—the study of knowledge—may itself

(60) lead to the discovery of new forms of knowledge about how the mind works.

According to the passage, subjectivists advance which one of the following claims to support their charge that objectivism is faulty?

(A) Objectivism rests on evidence that conflicts with the data of introspection.

*(B) Objectivism restricts the kinds of experience from which philosophers may draw knowledge.

(C) Objectivism relies on data that can be described and interpreted only by scientific specialists.

(D) Objectivism provides no context in which to view scientific data as relevant to philosophical questions.

(E) Objectivism concerns itself with questions that have not traditionally been part of philosophical inquiry.

The contemporary Mexican artistic movement known as muralism, a movement of public art that began with images painted on walls in an effort to represent Mexican national culture, is closely linked
(5) ideologically with its main sponsor, the new Mexican government elected in 1920 following the Mexican Revolution. This government promoted an ambitious cultural program, and the young revolutionary state called on artists to display Mexico's richness and
(10) possibility. But the theoretical foundation of the movement was formulated by the artists themselves. The major figures in the muralist movement, David Alfaro Siqueiros, Diego Rivera, and José Clemente Orozco, all based their work on a common premise:
(15) that art should incorporate images and familiar ideas as it commented upon the historic period in which it was created. In the process, they assimilated into their work the customs, myths, geography, and history of the local communities that constitute the basis of Mexican
(20) national culture.

But while many muralist works express populist or nationalist ideas, it is a mistake to attempt to reduce Mexican mural painting to formulaic, official government art. It is more than merely the result of the
(25) changes in political and social awareness that the Mexican Revolution represented; it also reflected important innovations in the art world. In creating a wide panorama of Mexico's history on the walls of public buildings throughout the country, muralists
(30) often used a realist style. But awareness of these innovations enabled them to be freer in expression than were more traditional practitioners of this style.

Moreover, while they shared a common interest in rediscovering their Mexican national identity, they
(35) developed their own distinct styles. Rivera, for example, incorporated elements from pre-Columbian sculpture and the Italian Renaissance fresco into his murals and used a strange combination of mechanical shapes to depict the faces and bodies of people.
(40) Orozco, on the other hand, showed a more expressionist approach, with loose brushwork and an openly emotional treatment of form. He relied on a strong diagonal line to give a sense of heightened movement and drama to his work. Siqueiros developed
(45) in a somewhat similar direction as Orozco, but incorporated asymmetric compositions, a high degree of action, and brilliant color.

This stylistic experimentation can be seen as resulting from the demands of a new medium. In
(50) stretching their concepts from small easel paintings with a centralized subject to vast compositions with mural dimensions, muralists learned to think big and to respect the sweeping gesture of the arm—the brush stroke required to achieve the desired bold effect of
(55) mural art. Furthermore, because they were painting murals, they thought in terms of a continuum; their works were designed to be viewable from many different vantage points, to have an equally strong impact in all parts, and to continue to be viewable as
(60) people moved across in front of them.

Until the 1980s, most scientists believed that noncatastrophic geological processes caused the extinction of dinosaurs that occurred approximately 66 million years ago, at the end of the Cretaceous period. Geologists argued that a dramatic drop in sea level coincided with the extinction of the dinosaurs and could have caused the climatic changes that resulted in this extinction as well as the extinction of many ocean species.

(5)

This view was seriously challenged in the 1980s by the discovery of large amounts of iridium in a layer of clay deposited at the end of the Cretaceous period. Because iridium is extremely rare in rocks on the Earth's surface but common in meteorites, researchers theorized that it was the impact of a large meteorite that dramatically changed the Earth's climate and thus triggered the extinction of the dinosaurs.

(10)

(15)

Currently available evidence, however, offers more support for a new theory, the volcanic-eruption theory. A vast eruption of lava in India coincided with the extinctions that occurred at the end of the Cretaceous period, and the release of carbon dioxide from this episode of volcanism could have caused the climatic change responsible for the demise of the dinosaurs. Such outpourings of lava are caused by instability in the lowest layer of the Earth's mantle, located just above the Earth's core. As the rock that constitutes this layer is heated by the Earth's core, it becomes less dense and portions of it eventually escape upward as blobs of molten rock, called "diapirs," that can, under certain circumstances, erupt violently through the Earth's crust.

(20)

(25)

(30)

Moreover, the volcanic-eruption theory, like the impact theory, accounts for the presence of iridium in sedimentary deposits; it also explains matters that the meteorite-impact theory does not. Although iridium is extremely rare on the Earth's surface, the lower regions of the Earth's mantle have roughly the same composition as meteorites and contain large amounts of iridium, which in the case of a diapir eruption would probably be emitted as iridium hexafluoride, a gas that would disperse more uniformly in the atmosphere than the iridium-containing matter thrown out from a meteorite impact. In addition, the volcanic-eruption theory may explain why the end of the Cretaceous period was marked by a gradual change in sea level.

(35)

(40)

(45)

Fossil records indicate that for several hundred thousand years prior to the relatively sudden disappearance of the dinosaurs, the level of the sea gradually fell, causing many marine organisms to die out. This change in sea level might well have been the result of a distortion in the Earth's surface that resulted from the movement of diapirs upward toward the Earth's crust, and the more cataclysmic extinction of the dinosaurs could have resulted from the explosive volcanism that occurred as material from the diapirs erupted onto the Earth's surface.

(50)

(55)

(60)

The law-and-literature movement claims to have introduced a valuable pedagogical innovation into legal study: instructing students in techniques of literary analysis for the purpose of interpreting laws and in the reciprocal use of legal analysis for the purpose of interpreting literary texts. The results, according to advocates, are not only conceptual breakthroughs in both law and literature but also more sensitive and humane lawyers. Whatever the truth of this last claim, there can be no doubt that the movement is a success: law-and-literature is an accepted subject in law journals and in leading law schools. Indeed, one indication of the movement's strength is the fact that its most distinguished critic, Richard A. Posner, paradoxically ends up expressing qualified support for the movement in a recent study in which he systematically refutes the writings of its leading legal scholars and cooperating literary critics.

Critiquing the movement's assumption that lawyers can offer special insights into literature that deals with legal matters, Posner points out that writers of literature use the law loosely to convey a particular idea, or as a metaphor for the workings of the society envisioned in their fiction. Legal questions per se, about which a lawyer might instruct readers, are seldom at issue in literature. This is why practitioners of law-and-literature end up discussing the law itself far less than one might suppose. Movement leader James White, for example, in his discussion of arguments in the *Iliad*, barely touches on law, and then so generally as to render himself vulnerable to Posner's devastating remark that "any argument can be analogized to a legal dispute."

Similarly, the notion that literary criticism can be helpful in interpreting law is problematic. Posner argues that literary criticism in general aims at exploring richness and variety of meaning in texts, whereas legal interpretation aims at discovering a single meaning. A literary approach can thus only confuse the task of interpreting the law, especially if one adopts current fashions like deconstruction, which holds that all texts are inherently uninterpretable.

Nevertheless, Posner writes that law-and-literature is a field with "promise." Why? Perhaps, recognizing the success of a movement that, in the past, has singled him out for abuse, he is attempting to appease his detractors, paying obeisance to the movement's institutional success by declaring that it "deserves a place in legal research" while leaving it to others to draw the conclusion from his cogent analysis that it is an entirely factitious undertaking, deserving of no intellectual respect whatsoever. As a result, his work stands both as a rebuttal of law-and-literature and as a tribute to the power it has come to exercise in academic circles.

Cultivation of a single crop on a given tract of land leads eventually to decreased yields. One reason for this is that harmful bacterial phytopathogens, organisms parasitic on plant hosts, increase in the soil surrounding plant roots. The problem can be cured by crop rotation, denying the pathogens a suitable host for a period of time. However, even if crops are not rotated, the severity of diseases brought on by such phytopathogens often decreases after a number of years as the microbial population of the soil changes and the soil becomes "suppressive" to those diseases. While there may be many reasons for this phenomenon, it is clear that levels of certain bacteria, such as *Pseudomonas fluorescens*, a bacterium antagonistic to a number of harmful phytopathogens, are greater in suppressive than in nonsuppressive soil. This suggests that the presence of such bacteria suppresses phytopathogens. There is now considerable experimental support for this view. Wheat yield increases of 27 percent have been obtained in field trials by treatment of wheat seeds with fluorescent pseudomonads. Similar treatment of sugar beets, cotton, and potatoes has had similar results.

These improvements in crop yields through the application of *Pseudomonas fluorescens* suggest that agriculture could benefit from the use of bacteria genetically altered for specific purposes. For example, a form of phytopathogen altered to remove its harmful properties could be released into the environment in quantities favorable to its competing with and eventually excluding the harmful normal strain. Some experiments suggest that deliberately releasing altered nonpathogenic *Pseudomonas syringae* could crowd out the nonaltered variety that causes frost damage. Opponents of such research have objected that the deliberate and large- scale release of genetically altered bacteria might have deleterious results. Proponents, on the other hand, argue that this particular strain is altered only by the removal of the gene responsible for the strain's propensity to cause frost damage, thereby rendering it safer than the phytopathogen from which it was derived.

Some proponents have gone further and suggest that genetic alteration techniques could create organisms with totally new combinations of desirable traits not found in nature. For example, genes responsible for production of insecticidal compounds have been transposed from other bacteria into pseudomonads that colonize corn roots. Experiments of this kind are difficult and require great care: such bacteria are developed in highly artificial environments and may not compete well with natural soil bacteria. Nevertheless, proponents contend that the prospects for improved agriculture through such methods seem excellent. These prospects lead many to hope that current efforts to assess the risks of deliberate release of altered microorganisms will successfully answer the concerns of opponents and create a climate in which such research can go forward without undue impediment.

Late-nineteenth-century books about the French artist Watteau (1684-1721) betray a curious blind spot: more than any single artist before or since, Watteau provided his age with an influential image of itself, and nineteenth-century writers accepted this image as genuine. This was largely due to the enterprise of Watteau's friends who, soon after his death, organized the printing of engraved reproductions of the great bulk of his work—both his paintings and his drawings—so that Watteau's total artistic output became and continued to be more accessible than that of any other artist until the twentieth-century advent of art monographs illustrated with photographs. These engravings presented aristocratic (and would-be aristocratic) eighteenth-century French society with an image of itself that was highly acceptable and widely imitated by other artists, however little relationship that image bore to reality. By 1884, the bicentenary of Watteau's birth, it was standard practice for biographers to refer to him as "the personification of the witty and amiable eighteenth century."

In fact, Watteau saw little enough of that "witty and amiable" century for which so much nostalgia was generally felt between about 1870 and 1920, a period during which enthusiasm for the artist reached its peak. The eighteenth century's first decades, the period of his artistic activity, were fairly calamitous ones. During his short life, France was almost continually at war: his native region was overrun with foreign troops, and Paris was threatened by siege and by a rampaging army rabble. The dreadful winter of 1709, the year of Watteau's first Paris successes, was marked by military defeat and a disastrous famine.

Most of Watteau's nineteenth-century admirers simply ignored the grim background of the works they found so lyrical and charming. Those who took the inconvenient historical facts into consideration did so only in order to refute the widely held deterministic view that the content and style of an artist's work were absolutely dictated by heredity and environment. (For Watteau admirers, such determinism was unthinkable: the artist was born in a Flemish town only six years after it first became part of France, yet Watteau was quintessentially French. As one patriotic French biographer put it, "In Dresden, Potsdam, and Berlin I have never come across a Watteau without feeling refreshed by a breath of native air.") Even such writers, however, persisted in according Watteau's canvases a privileged status as representative "personifications" of the eighteenth century. The discrepancy between historical fact and artistic vision, useful in refuting the extreme deterministic position, merely forced these writers to seek a new formula that allowed them to preserve the desired identity between image and reality, this time a rather suspiciously psychic one: Watteau did not record the society he knew, but rather "foresaw" a society that developed shortly after his death.

It can be inferred from the passage that the author's view of Watteau's works differs most significantly from that of most late-nineteenth-century Watteau admirers in which one of the following ways?

(A) Unlike most late-nineteenth-century Watteau admirers, the author appreciates the importance of Watteau's artistic accomplishment.

(B) The author finds Watteau's works to be much less lyrical and charming than did most late-nineteenth-century admirers of the works.

*(C) In contrast to most late-nineteenth-century Watteau admirers, the author finds it misleading to see Watteau's works as accurately reflecting social reality.

(D) The author is much more willing to entertain deterministic explanations of the origins of Watteau's works than were most late-nineteenth-century Watteau admirers.

(E) Unlike most late-nineteenth-century admirers of Watteau, the author considers it impossible for any work of art to personify or represent a particular historical period.

Oil companies need offshore platforms primarily because the oil or natural gas the companies extract from the ocean floor has to be processed before pumps can be used to move the substances ashore.

(5) But because processing crude (unprocessed oil or gas) on a platform rather than at facilities onshore exposes workers to the risks of explosion and to an unpredictable environment, researchers are attempting to diminish the need for human labor

(10) on platforms and even to eliminate platforms altogether by redesigning two kinds of pumps to handle crude. These pumps could then be used to boost the natural pressure driving the flow of crude, which, by itself, is sufficient only to bring

(15) the crude to the platform, located just above the wellhead. Currently, pumps that could boost this natural pressure sufficiently to drive the crude through a pipeline to the shore do not work consistently because of the crude's content. Crude

(20) may consist of oil or natural gas in multiphase states—combinations of liquids, gases, and solids under pressure—that do not reach the wellhead in constant proportions. The flow of crude oil, for example, can change quickly from 60 percent liquid

(25) to 70 percent gas. This surge in gas content causes loss of "head," or pressure inside a pump, with the result that a pump can no longer impart enough energy to transport the crude mixture through the pipeline and to the shore.

(30) Of the two pumps being redesigned, the positive-displacement pump is promising because it is immune to sudden shifts in the proportion of liquid to gas in the crude mixture. But the pump's design, which consists of a single or twin screw

(35) pushing the fluid from one end of the pump to the other, brings crude into close contact with most parts of the pump, and thus requires that it be made of expensive, corrosion-resistant material. The alternative is the centrifugal pump, which has a

(40) rotating impeller that sucks fluid in at one end and forces fluid out at the other. Although this pump has a proven design and has worked for years with little maintenance in waste-disposal plants, researchers have discovered that because the swirl

(45) of its impeller separates gas out from the oil that normally accompanies it, significant reductions in head can occur as it operates.

Research in the development of these pumps is focused mainly on trying to reduce the cost of the

(50) positive-displacement pump and attempting to make the centrifugal pump more tolerant of gas. Other researchers are looking at ways of adapting either kind of pump for use underwater, so that crude could be moved directly from the sea bottom

(55) to processing facilities onshore, eliminating platforms.

Although surveys of medieval legislation, guild organization, and terminology used to designate different medical practitioners have demonstrated that numerous medical specialties were recognized
(5) in Europe during the Middle Ages, most historians continue to equate the term "woman medical practitioner," wherever they encounter it in medieval records, with "midwife." This common practice obscures the fact that, although women
(10) were not represented on all levels of medicine equally, they were represented in a variety of specialties throughout the broad medical community. A reliable study by Wickersheimer and Jacquart documents that, of 7,647 medical practitioners in
(15) France during the twelfth through fifteenth centuries, 121 were women; of these, only 44 were identified as midwives, while the rest practiced as physicians, surgeons, apothecaries, barbers, and other healers.

While preserving terminological distinctions
(20) somewhat increases the quality of the information extracted from medieval documents concerning women medical practitioners, scholars must also reopen the whole question of why documentary evidence for women medical practitioners
(25) comprises such a tiny fraction of the evidence historians of medieval medicine usually present. Is this due to the limitations of the historical record, as has been claimed, or does it also result from the methods historians use? Granted, apart from
(30) medical licenses, the principal sources of information regarding medical practitioners available to researchers are wills, property transfers, court records, and similar documents, all of which typically underrepresent women because of
(35) restrictive medieval legal traditions. Nonetheless, the parameters researchers choose when they define their investigations may contribute to the problem. Studies focusing on the upper echelons of "learned" medicine, for example, tend to exclude healers on
(40) the legal and social fringes of medical practice, where most women would have been found.

The advantages of broadening the scope of such studies is immediately apparent in Pelling and Webster's study of sixteenth-century London.
(45) Instead of focusing solely on officially recognized and licensed practitioners, the researchers defined a medical practitioner as "any individual whose occupation is basically concerned with the care of the sick." Using this definition, they found primary

(50) source information suggesting that there were 60 women medical practitioners in the city of London in 1560. Although this figure may be slightly exaggerated, the evidence contrasts strikingly with that of Gottfried, whose earlier survey identified
(55) only 28 women medical practitioners in all of England between 1330 and 1530.

Finally, such studies provide only statistical information about the variety and prevalence of women's medical practice in medieval Europe.
(60) Future studies might also make profitable use of analyses developed in other areas of women's history as a basis for exploring the social context of women's medical practice. Information about economic rivalry in medicine, women's literacy, and
(65) the control of medical knowledge could add much to our growing understanding of women medical practitioners' role in medieval society.

Critics have long been puzzled by the inner contradictions of major characters in John Webster's tragedies. In his *The Duchess of Malfi*, for instance, the Duchess is "good" in demonstrating
(5) the obvious tenderness and sincerity of her love for Antonio, but "bad" in ignoring the wishes and welfare of her family and in making religion a "cloak" hiding worldly self-indulgence. Bosola is "bad" in serving Ferdinand, "good" in turning the
(10) Duchess' thoughts toward heaven and in planning to avenge her murder. The ancient Greek philosopher Aristotle implied that such contradictions are virtually essential to the tragic personality, and yet critics keep coming back to this element of
(15) inconsistency as though it were an eccentric feature of Webster's own tragic vision.

The problem is that, as an Elizabethan playwright, Webster has become a prisoner of our critical presuppositions. We have, in recent years, been
(20) dazzled by the way the earlier Renaissance and medieval theater, particularly the morality play, illuminates Elizabethan drama. We now understand how the habit of mind that saw the world as a battleground between good and evil produced the
(25) morality play. Morality plays allegorized that conflict by presenting characters whose actions were defined as the embodiment of good or evil. This model of reality lived on, overlaid by different conventions, in the more sophisticated Elizabethan
(30) works of the following age. Yet Webster seems not to have been as heavily influenced by the morality play's model of reality as were his Elizabethan contemporaries; he was apparently more sensitive to the more morally complicated Italian drama
(35) than to these English sources. Consequently, his characters cannot be evaluated according to reductive formulas of good and evil, which is precisely what modern critics have tried to do. They choose what seem to be the most promising of the
(40) contradictory values that are dramatized in the play, and treat those values as if they were the only basis for analyzing the moral development of the play's major characters, attributing the inconsistencies in a character's behavior to artistic
(45) incompetence on Webster's part. The lack of consistency in Webster's characters can be better understood if we recognize that the ambiguity at the heart of his tragic vision lies not in the external world but in the duality of human nature. Webster

(50) establishes tension in his plays by setting up conflicting systems of value that appear immoral only when one value system is viewed exclusively from the perspective of the other. He presents us not only with characters that we condemn
(55) intellectually or ethically and at the same time impulsively approve of, but also with judgments we must accept as logically sound and yet find emotionally repulsive. The dilemma is not only dramatic: it is tragic, because the conflict is
(60) irreconcilable, and because it is ours as much as that of the characters.

During the 1940s and 1950s the United States government developed a new policy toward Native Americans, often known as "readjustment." Because the increased awareness of civil rights in
(5) these decades helped reinforce the belief that life on reservations prevented Native Americans from exercising the rights guaranteed to citizens under the United States Constitution, the readjustment movement advocated the end of the federal
(10) government's involvement in Native American and encouraged the assimilation of Native Americans as individuals into mainstream society. However, the same years also saw the emergence of a Native American leadership and efforts to develop
(15) tribal institutions and reaffirm tribal identity. The clash of these two trends may be traced in the attempts on the part of the Bureau of Indian Affairs (BIA) to convince the Oneida tribe of Wisconsin to accept readjustment.
(20) The culmination of BIA efforts to sway the Oneida occurred at a meeting that took place in the fall of 1956. The BIA suggested that it would be to the Oneida's benefit to own their own property and, like other homeowners, pay real estate taxes
(25) on it. The BIA also emphasized that, after readjustment, the government would not attempt to restrict Native Americans' ability to sell their individually owned lands. The Oneida were then offered a one-time lump-sum payment of $60,000 in
(30) lieu of the $0.52 annuity guaranteed in perpetuity to each member of the tribe under the Canandaigua Treaty.
The efforts of the BIA to "sell" readjustment to the tribe failed because the Oneida realized that
(35) they had heard similar offers before. The Oneida delegates reacted negatively to the BIA's first suggestion because taxation of Native American lands had been one past vehicle for dispossessing the Oneida: after the distribution of some tribal
(40) lands to individual Native Americans in the late nineteenth century, Native American lands became subject to taxation, resulting in new and impossible financial burdens, foreclosures, and subsequent tax sales of property. The Oneida delegates were
(45) equally suspicious of the BIA's emphasis on the rights of individual landowners, since in the late nineteenth century many individual Native Americans had been convinced by unscrupulous speculators to sell their lands. Finally, the offer of a

(50) lump-sum payment was unanimously opposed by the Oneida delegates, who saw that changing the terms of a treaty might jeopardize the many pending land claims based upon the treaty.
As a result of the 1956 meeting, the Oneida
(55) rejected readjustment. Instead, they determined to improve tribal life by lobbying for federal monies for postsecondary education, for the improvement of drainage on tribal lands, and for the building of a convalescent home for tribal members. Thus, by
(60) learning the lessons of history, the Oneida were able to survive as a tribe in their homeland.

For too many years scholars of African American history focused on the harm done by slaveholders and by the institution of slavery, rather than on what Africans in the United States were able to accomplish despite the effects of that institution. In *Myne Owne Ground*, T. H. Breen and Stephen Innes contribute significantly to a recent, welcome shift from a white-centered to a black-centered inquiry into the role of African Americans in the American colonial period. Breen and Innes focus not on slaves, but on a small group of freed indentured servants in Northampton County (in the Chesapeake Bay region of Virginia) who, according to the authors, maintained their freedom, secured property, and interacted with persons of different races and economic standing from 1620 through the 1670s. African Americans living on the Chesapeake were to some extent disadvantaged, say Breen and Innes, but this did not preclude the attainment of status roughly equal to that of certain white planters of the area. Continuously acting within black social networks, and forming economic relationships with white planters, local Native Americans, indentured servants, and white settlers outside the gentry class, the free African Americans of Northampton County held their own in the rough-hewn world of Chesapeake Bay.

The authors emphasize that in this early period, when the percentage of African Americans in any given Chesapeake county was still no more than 10 percent of the population, very little was predetermined so far as racial status or race relations were concerned. By schooling themselves in the local legal process and by working prodigiously on the land, African Americans acquired property, established families, and warded off contentious white neighbors. Breen and Innes do acknowledge that political power on the Chesapeake was asymmetrically distributed among black and white residents. However, they underemphasize much evidence that customary law, only gradually embodied in statutory law, was closing in on free African Americans well before the 1670s: during the 1660s, when the proportion of African Americans in Virginia increased dramatically, Virginia tightened a law regulating interracial relations (1662) and enacted a statute prohibiting baptism from altering slave status (1667). Anthony Johnson, a leader in the community of free African Americans in the Chesapeake Bay region, sold the land he had cultivated for more than twenty years and moved north with his family around 1665, an action that the authors attribute to a search for "fresh, more productive land." But the answer to why the Johnsons left that area where they had labored so long may lie in their realization that their white neighbors were already beginning the transition from a largely white indentured labor force to reliance on a largely black slave labor force, and that the institution of slavery was threatening their descendants' chances for freedom and success in Virginia.

A recent generation of historians of science, far from portraying accepted scientific views as objectively accurate reflections of a natural world, explain the acceptance of such views in terms of the (5) ideological biases of certain influential scientists or the institutional and rhetorical power such scientists wield. As an example of ideological bias, it has been argued that Pasteur rejected the theory of spontaneous generation not because of (10) experimental evidence but because he rejected the materialist ideology implicit in that doctrine. These historians seem to find allies in certain philosophers of science who argue that scientific views are not imposed by reality but are free inventions of (15) creative minds, and that scientific claims are never more than brave conjectures, always subject to inevitable future falsification. While these philosophers of science themselves would not be likely to have much truck with the recent historians (20) it is an easy step from their views to the extremism of the historians.

While this rejection of the traditional belief that scientific views are objective reflections of the world may be fashionable, it is deeply implausible. We (25) now know, for example, that water is made of hydrogen and oxygen and that parents each contribute one-half of their children's complement of genes. I do not believe any serious-minded and informed person can claim that these statements are (30) not factual descriptions of the world or that they will inevitably be falsified.

However, science's accumulation of lasting truths about the world is not by any means a straightforward matter. We certainly need to (35) get beyond the naïve view that the truth will automatically reveal itself to any scientist who looks in the right direction; most often, in fact, a whole series of prior discoveries is needed to tease reality's truths from experiment and observation. (40) And the philosophers of science mentioned above are quite right to argue that new scientific ideas often correct old ones by indicating errors and imprecisions (as, say, Newton's ideas did to Kepler's). Nor would I deny that there are (45) interesting questions to be answered about the social processes in which scientific activity is embedded. The persuasive processes by which particular scientific groups establish their experimental results as authoritative are themselves (50) social activities and can be rewardingly studied as such. Indeed, much of the new work in the history of science has been extremely revealing about the institutional interactions and rhetorical devices that help determine whose results achieve prominence.

(55) But one can accept all this without accepting the thesis that natural reality never plays any part at all in determining what scientists believe. What the new historians ought to be showing us is how those doctrines that do in fact fit reality work their way (60) through the complex social processes of scientific activity to eventually receive general scientific acceptance.

A major tenet of the neurosciences has been that all neurons (nerve cells) in the brains of vertebrate animals are formed early in development. An adult vertebrate, it was believed, must make do with a
(5) fixed number of neurons: those lost through disease or injury are not replaced, and adult learning takes place not through generation of new cells but through modification of connections among existing ones.

(10) However, new evidence for neurogenesis (the birth of new neurons) has come from the study of canary song. Young canaries and other songbirds learn to sing much as humans learn to speak, by imitating models provided by their elders. Several
(15) weeks after birth, a young bird produces its first rudimentary attempts at singing; over the next few months the song becomes more structured and stable, reaching a fully developed state by the time the bird approaches its first breeding season. But
(20) this repertoire of song is not permanently learned. After each breeding season, during late summer and fall, the bird loses mastery of its developed "vocabulary," and its song becomes as unstable as that of a juvenile bird. During the following winter
(25) and spring, however, the canary acquires new songs, and by the next breeding season it has developed an entirely new repertoire.

Recent neurological research into this learning and relearning process has shown that the two most
(30) important regions of the canary's brain related to the learning of songs actually vary in size at different times of the year. In the spring, when the bird's song is highly developed and uniform, the regions are roughly twice as large as they are in the
(35) fall. Further experiments tracing individual nerve cells within these regions have shown that the number of neurons drops by about 38 percent after the breeding season, but by the following breeding season, new ones have been generated to replace
(40) them. A possible explanation for this continual replacement of nerve cells may have to do with the canary's relatively long life span and the requirements of flight. Its brain would have to be substantially larger and heavier than might be
(45) feasible for flying if it had to carry all the brain cells needed to process and retain all the information gathered over a lifetime.

Although the idea of neurogenesis in the adult mammalian brain is still not generally accepted,
(50) these findings might help uncover a mechanism that would enable the human brain to repair itself through neurogenesis. Whether such replacement of neurons would disrupt complex learning processes or long-term memory is not known, but
(55) songbird research challenges scientists to identify the genes or hormones that orchestrate neurogenesis in the young human brain and to learn how to activate them in the adult brain.

The following passages concern a plant called purple loosestrife. Passage A is excerpted from a report issued by a prairie research council; passage B from a journal of sociology.

Passage A

Purple loosestrife (Lythrum salicaria), an aggressive and invasive perennial of Eurasian origin, arrived with settlers in eastern North America in the early 1800s and has spread across the continent's
(5) midlatitude wetlands. The impact of purple loosestrife on native vegetation has been disastrous, with more than 50 percent of the biomass of some wetland communities displaced. Monospecific blocks of this weed have maintained themselves for at least 20 years.
(10) Impacts on wildlife have not been well studied, but serious reductions in waterfowl and aquatic furbearer productivity have been observed. In addition, several endangered species of vertebrates are threatened with further degradation of their
(15) breeding habitats. Although purple loosestrife can invade relatively undisturbed habitats, the spread and dominance of this weed have been greatly accelerated in disturbed habitats. While digging out the plants can temporarily halt their spread, there has been little
(20) research on long-term purple loosestrife control. Glyphosate has been used successfully, but no measure of the impact of this herbicide on native plant communities has been made.

With the spread of purple loosestrife growing
(25) exponentially, some form of integrated control is needed. At present, coping with purple loosestrife hinges on early detection of the weed's arrival in areas, which allows local eradication to be carried out with minimum damage to the native plant community.

Passage B

(30) The war on purple loosestrife is apparently conducted on behalf of nature, an attempt to liberate the biotic community from the tyrannical influence of a life-destroying invasive weed. Indeed, purple loosestrife control is portrayed by its practitioners as
(35) an environmental initiative intended to save nature rather than control it. Accordingly, the purple loosestrife literature, scientific and otherwise, dutifully discusses the impacts of the weed on endangered species—and on threatened biodiversity
(40) more generally. Purple loosestrife is a pollution, according to the scientific community, and all of nature suffers under its pervasive influence.

Regardless of the perceived and actual ecological effects of the purple invader, it is apparent that
(45) popular pollution ideologies have been extended into the wetlands of North America. Consequently, the scientific effort to liberate nature from purple loosestrife has failed to decouple itself from its philosophical origin as an instrument to control nature
(50) to the satisfaction of human desires. Birds, particularly game birds and waterfowl, provide the bulk of the justification for loosestrife management. However, no bird species other than the canvasback has been identified in the literature as endangered by
(55) purple loosestrife. The impact of purple loosestrife on furbearing mammals is discussed at great length, though none of the species highlighted (muskrat, mink) can be considered threatened in North America. What is threatened by purple loosestrife is the
(60) economics of exploiting such preferred species and the millions of dollars that will be lost to the economies of the United States and Canada from reduced hunting, trapping, and recreation revenues due to a decline in the production of the wetland
(65) resource.

The following passages are adapted from critical essays on the American writer Willa Cather (1873–1947).

Passage A

When Cather gave examples of high quality in fiction, she invariably cited Russian writers I van Turgenev or Leo Tolstoy or both. Indeed,
(5) Edmund Wilson noted in 1922 that Cather followed the manner of Turgenev, not depicting her characters' emotions directly but telling us how they behave and letting their "inner blaze of glory shine through the simple recital." Turgenev's method was to select details that described a character's appearance and
(10) actions without trying to explain them. A writer, he said, "must be a psychologist—but a secret one; he must know and feel the roots of phenomena, but only present the phenomena themselves." Similarly, he argued that a writer must have complete knowledge
(15) of a character so as to avoid overloading the work with unnecessary detail, concentrating instead on what is characteristic and typical.

Here we have an impressionistic aesthetic that anticipates Cather's: what Turgenev referred to as
(20) secret knowledge Cather called "the thing not named." In one essay she writes that "whatever is felt upon the page without being specifically named there—that, one might say, is created." For both writers, there is the absolute importance of selection and simplification;
(25) for both, art is the fusing of the physical world of setting and actions with the emotional reality of the characters. What synthesizes all the elements of narrative for these writers is the establishment of a prevailing mood.

Passage B

(30) In a famous 1927 letter, Cather writes of her novel *Death Comes for the Archbishop*, "Many [reviewers] assert vehemently that it is not a novel. Myself, I prefer to call it a narrative." Cather's preference anticipated an important reformulation of
(35) the criticism of fiction: the body of literary theory, called "narratology," articulated by French literary theorists in the 1960s. This approach broadens and simplifies the fundamental paradigms according to which we view fiction: they ask of narrative only that
(40) it be narrative, that it tell a story. Narratologists tend not to focus on the characteristics of narrative's dominant modern Western form, the "realistic novel": direct psychological characterization, realistic treatment of time, causal plotting, logical closure.
(45) Such a model of criticism, which takes as its object "narrative" rather than the "novel," seems exactly appropriate to Cather's work.

Indeed, her severest critics have always questioned precisely her capabilities as a novelist. Morton Zabel
(50) argued that "[Cather's] themes...could readily fail to find the structure and substance that might have given them life or redeemed them from the tenuity of a sketch"; Leon Edel called one of her novels "two inconclusive fragments." These critics and others like
(55) them treat as failures some of the central features of Cather's impressionistic technique: unusual treatment of narrative time, unexpected focus, ambiguous conclusions, a preference for the bold, simple, and stylized in character as well as in landscape. These
(60) "non-novelistic" structures indirectly articulate the essential and conflicting forces of desire at work throughout Cather's fiction.

The following passages on freedom of information are adapted from texts published in the United Kingdom.

Passage A

We have made a commitment to openness in government, and now it is essential that we strengthen that commitment with legislation that guarantees public access to government information. This is something
(5) that the previous Government conspicuously failed to do. What resulted was a haphazard approach based largely on nonstatutory arrangements, in particular the Code of Practice on Access to Government Information. Those statutory requirements for openness
(10) that were in place applied only in certain areas, such as environmental information, or were limited to particular sectors of the public service.

We could have scored an early legislative achievement by simply enacting the Code of Practice
(15) into law, but it does not ultimately provide a satisfactory guarantee of openness. Some of its significant drawbacks, which our proposed legislation seeks to remedy, are that:

- it contains too many exemptions—more than
(20) any of the main statutory freedom of information regimes elsewhere in the world. This inevitably makes it complex for applicants to use, and encourages accusations that Departments "trawl" for possible reasons
(25) for nondisclosure.
- its wording encourages the use of a "category-based" approach toward exemptions by which whole classes of information or records are protected against disclosure,
(30) leaving no scope for partial disclosure of documents of those types (after deletion of sensitive material);
- it often requires assessing the relative weights to be assigned to the harm that a disclosure
(35) could cause and the public interest in disclosure. But the "public interest" is not defined, making it difficult for government staff, as well as for those who may be unfamiliar with the Code and with effective
(40) disclosure practices, to assess what would constitute harm to that interest.

Passage B

There is, of course, room for disagreement as to how best to achieve freedom of information, but there are a number of features common to all genuinely
(45) successful freedom of information regimes. The statute (or other legal instrument) creating the regime must contain a general presumption in favor of disclosure. There must be a general right of access to information held by public authorities that relates to their public
(50) functions. This right must be made subject to exemptions in order to protect specified public interests such as public health or public safety. These interests must, however, be narrowly drawn and disclosure refused only where it can be shown that disclosure of
(55) the particular piece of information withheld would cause harm to one or more of those interests. Many advocates of freedom of information would add that even where there is potential harm to a specified interest, disclosure should only be refused where the
(60) harm can be shown to outweigh the public's interest in disclosure of the information in question. Lastly, there must be the possibility of appeal to an independent body or official against refusals by public authorities to disclose information. This body or official must have
(65) the power to redetermine applications independently and to make binding decisions.

Passage A

Readers, like writers, need to search for answers. Part of the joy of reading is in being surprised, but academic historians leave little to the imagination. The perniciousness of the historiographic approach became
(5) fully evident to me when I started teaching. Historians require undergraduates to read scholarly monographs that sap the vitality of history; they visit on students what was visited on them in graduate school. They assign books with formulaic arguments that transform
(10) history into an abstract debate that would have been unfathomable to those who lived in the past. Aimed so squarely at the head, such books cannot stimulate students who yearn to connect to history emotionally as well as intellectually.
(15) In an effort to address this problem, some historians have begun to rediscover stories. It has even become something of a fad within the profession. This year, the American Historical Association chose as the theme for its annual conference some putative connection to
(20) storytelling: "Practices of Historical Narrative." Predictably, historians responded by adding the word "narrative" to their titles and presenting papers at sessions on "Oral History and the Narrative of Class Identity," and "Meaning and Time: The Problem of
(25) Historical Narrative." But it was still historiography, intended only for other academics. At meetings of historians, we still encounter very few historians telling stories or moving audiences to smiles, chills, or tears.

Passage B

Writing is at the heart of the lawyer's craft, and so,
(30) like it or not, we who teach the law inevitably teach aspiring lawyers how lawyers write. We do this in a few stand-alone courses and, to a greater extent, through the constraints that we impose on their writing throughout the curriculum. Legal writing, because of the purposes
(35) it serves, is necessarily ruled by linear logic, creating a path without diversions, surprises, or reversals. Conformity is a virtue, creativity suspect, humor forbidden, and voice mute.

Lawyers write as they see other lawyers write, and,
(40) influenced by education, profession, economic constraints, and perceived self-interest, they too often write badly. Perhaps the currently fashionable call for attention to narrative in legal education could have an effect on this. It is not yet exactly clear what role
(45) narrative should play in the law, but it is nonetheless true that every case has at its heart a story—of real events and people, of concerns, misfortunes, conflicts, feelings. But because legal analysis strips the human narrative content from the abstract, canonical legal
(50) form of the case, law students learn to act as if there is no such story.

It may well turn out that some of the terminology and public rhetoric of this potentially subversive movement toward attention to narrative will find its
(55) way into the law curriculum, but without producing corresponding changes in how legal writing is actually taught or in how our future colleagues will write. Still, even mere awareness of the value of narrative could perhaps serve as an important corrective.

Passage A

Drilling fluids, including the various mixtures known as drilling muds, play essential roles in oil-well drilling. As they are circulated down through the drill pipe and back up the well itself, they lubricate the
(5) drill bit, bearings, and drill pipe; clean and cool the drill bit as it cuts into the rock; lift rock chips (cuttings) to the surface; provide information about what is happening downhole, allowing the drillers to monitor the behavior, flow rate, pressure, and
(10) composition of the drilling fluid; and maintain well pressure to control cave-ins.

Drilling muds are made of bentonite and other clays and polymers, mixed with a fluid to the desired viscosity. By far the largest ingredient of drilling
(15) muds, by weight, is barite, a very heavy mineral of density 4.3 to 4.6. It is also used as an inert filler in some foods and is more familiar in its medical use as the "barium meal" administered before X-raying the digestive tract.
(20) Over the years individual drilling companies and their expert drillers have devised proprietary formulations, or mud "recipes," to deal with specific types of drilling jobs. One problem in studying the effects of drilling waste discharges is that the drilling
(25) fluids are made from a range of over 1,000, sometimes toxic, ingredients—many of them known, confusingly, by different trade names, generic descriptions, chemical formulae, and regional or industry slang words, and many of them kept secret by companies or individual
(30) formulators.

Passage B

Drilling mud, cuttings, and associated chemicals are normally released only during the drilling phase of a well's existence. These discharges are the main environmental concern in offshore oil production, and
(35) their use is tightly regulated. The discharges are closely monitored by the offshore operator, and releases are controlled as a condition of the operating permit.

One type of mud—water-based mud (WBM)—is a mixture of water, bentonite clay, and chemical
(40) additives, and is used to drill shallow parts of wells. It is not particularly toxic to marine organisms and disperses readily. Under current regulations, it can be dumped directly overboard. Companies typically recycle WBMs until their properties are no longer
(45) suitable and then, over a period of hours, dump the entire batch into the sea.

For drilling deeper wells, oil-based mud (OBM) is normally used. The typical difference from WBM is the high content of mineral oil (typically 30 percent).

(50) OBMs also contain greater concentrations of barite, a powdered heavy mineral, and a number of additives. OBMs have a greater potential for negative environmental impact, partly because they do not disperse as readily. Barite may impact some
(55) organisms, particularly scallops, and the mineral oil may have toxic effects. Currently only the residues of OBMs adhering to cuttings that remain after the cuttings are sieved from the drilling fluids may be discharged overboard, and then only mixtures up to a
(60) specified maximum oil content.

According to passage B, one reason OBMs are potentially more environmentally damaging than WBMs is that OBMs

*(A) are slower to disperse
(B) contain greater concentrations of bentonite
(C) contain a greater number of additives
(D) are used for drilling deeper wells
(E) cannot be recycled

Which one of the following is a characteristic of barite that is mentioned in both of the passages?

(A) It does not disperse readily in seawater.
(B) It is not found in drilling muds containing bentonite.
(C) Its use in drilling muds is tightly regulated.
(D) It is the most commonly used ingredient in drilling muds.
*(E) It is a heavy mineral.

Passage A

There is no universally accepted definition within international law for the term "national minority." It is most commonly applied to (1) groups of persons—not necessarily citizens—under the jurisdiction of one (5) country who have ethnic ties to another "homeland" country, or (2) groups of citizens of a country who have lasting ties to that country and have no such ties to any other country, but are distinguished from the majority of the population by ethnicity, religion, or (10) language. The terms "people" and "nation" are also vaguely defined in international agreements. Documents that refer to a "nation" generally link the term to the concept of "nationalism," which is often associated with ties to land. It also connotes sovereignty, for (15) which reason, perhaps, "people" is often used instead of "nation" for groups subject to a colonial power.

While the lack of definition of the terms "minority," "people," and "nation" presents difficulties to numerous minority groups, this lack is particularly problematic (20) for the Roma (Gypsies). The Roma are not a colonized people, they do not have a homeland, and many do not bear ties to any currently existing country. Some Roma are not even citizens of any country, in part because of their nomadic way of life, which developed in response (25) to centuries of fleeing persecution. Instead, they have ethnic and linguistic ties to other groups of Roma that reside in other countries.

Passage B

Capotorti's definition of a minority includes four empirical criteria—a group's being numerically smaller (30) than the rest of the population of the state; their being nondominant; their having distinctive ethnic, linguistic, or religious characteristics; and their desiring to preserve their own culture—and one legal criterion, that they be citizens of the state in question. This last (35) element can be problematic, given the previous nomadic character of the Roma, that they still cross borders between European states to avoid persecution, and that some states have denied them citizenship, and thus minority status. Because this element essentially (40) grants the state the arbitrary right to decide if the Roma constitute a minority without reference to empirical characteristics, it seems patently unfair that it should be included in the definition.

However, the Roma easily fulfill the four (45) objective elements of Capotorti's definition and should, therefore, be considered a minority in all major European states. Numerically, they are nowhere near a majority, though they number in the hundreds of thousands, even millions, in some states. Their (50) nondominant position is evident—they are not even acknowledged as a minority in some states. The Roma have a number of distinctive linguistic, ethnic, and religious characteristics. For example, most speak Romani, an Indo-European language descended from (55) Sanskrit. Roma groups also have their own distinctive legal and court systems, which are group oriented rather than individual-rights oriented. That they have preserved their language, customs, and identity through centuries of persecution is evidence enough (60) of their desire to preserve their culture.

Which one of the following most accurately expresses the main point of passage A?

(A) Different definitions of certain key terms in international law conflict with one another in their application to the Roma.

(B) In at least some countries in which they live, the Roma are not generally considered a minority group.

(C) The lack of agreement regarding the definitions of such terms as "minority," "people," and "nation" is partly due to the unclear application of the terms to groups such as the Roma.

(D) Any attempt to define such concepts as people, nation, or minority group will probably fail to apply to certain borderline cases such as the Roma.

*(E) The absence of a clear, generally agreed-upon understanding of what constitutes a people, nation, or minority group is a problem, especially in relation to the Roma.

The term "problematic" has which one of the following meanings in both passage A (line 19) and passage B (line 35)?

(A) giving rise to intense debate
(B) confusing and unclear
*(C) resulting in difficulties
(D) difficult to solve
(E) theoretically incoherent

The following passages were adapted from articles published in the mid-1990s.

Passage A

In January 1995 a vast section of ice broke off the Larsen ice shelf in Antarctica. While this occurrence, the direct result of a regional warming trend that began in the 1940s, may be the most spectacular
(5) manifestation yet of serious climate changes occurring on the planet as a consequence of atmospheric heating, other symptoms—more intense storms, prolonged droughts, extended heat waves, and record flooding—have been emerging around the
(10) world for several years.

According to scientific estimates, furthermore, sea-level rise resulting from global warming will reach 3 feet (1 meter) within the next century. Such a rise could submerge vast coastal areas, with
(15) potentially irreversible consequences.

Late in 1995 the Intergovernmental Panel on Climate Change (IPCC) reported that it had detected the "fingerprint" of human activity as a contributor to the warming of the earth's atmosphere. Furthermore,
(20) panel scientists attributed such warming directly to the increasing quantities of carbon dioxide released by our burning of fossil fuels. The IPCC report thus clearly identifies a pattern of climatic response to human activities in the climatological record, thereby
(25) establishing without doubt that global warming can no longer be attributed solely to natural climate variability.

Passage B

Over the past two decades, an extreme view of global warming has developed. While it contains
(30) some facts, this view also contains exaggerations and misstatements, and has sometimes resulted in unreasonable environmental policies.

According to this view, global warming will cause the polar ice to melt, raising global sea levels,
(35) flooding entire regions, destroying crops, and displacing millions of people. However, there is still a great deal of uncertainty regarding a potential rise in sea levels. Certainly, if the earth warms, sea levels will rise as the water heats up and expands. If the
(40) polar ice caps melt, more water will be added to the oceans, raising sea levels even further. There is some evidence that melting has occurred; however, there is also evidence that the Antarctic ice sheets are growing. In fact, it is possible that a warmer sea-

(45) surface temperature will cause more water to evaporate, and when wind carries the moisture-laden air over the land, it will precipitate out as snow, causing the ice sheets to grow. Certainly, we need to have better knowledge about the hydrological cycle
(50) before predicting dire consequences as a result of recent increases in global temperatures.

This view also exaggerates the impact that human activity has on the planet. While human activity may be a factor in global warming, natural events appear
(55) to be far more important. The 1991 eruption of Mount Pinatubo in the Philippines, for example, caused a decrease in the average global temperature, while El Niño, a periodic perturbation in the ocean's temperature and circulation, causes extreme global
(60) climatic events, including droughts and major flooding. Of even greater importance to the earth's climate are variations in the sun's radiation and in the earth's orbit. Climate variability has always existed and will continue to do so, regardless of human
(65) intervention.

The author of passage A would be most likely to agree with which one of the following assertions from passage B?

(A) More complete knowledge is needed before severe consequences from warming trends can be predicted.
(B) Climate variability is a more important factor than human activity in global warming.
(C) Evidence suggests that the Antarctic ice sheets are growing rather than shrinking in size.
(D) Whether millions of people will be displaced by rising global sea levels is uncertain.
*(E) A reduction in the size of the polar ice caps would cause sea levels to rise.

Passage A

Did music and human language originate separately or together? Both systems use intonation and rhythm to communicate emotions. Both can be produced vocally or with tools, and people can produce
(5) both music and language silently to themselves.

Brain imaging studies suggest that music and language are part of one large, vastly complicated, neurological system for processing sound. In fact, fewer differences than similarities exist between the
(10) neurological processing of the two. One could think of the two activities as different radio programs that can be broadcast over the same hardware. One noteworthy difference, though, is that, generally speaking, people are better at language than music. In music, anyone
(15) can listen easily enough, but most people do not perform well, and in many cultures composition is left to specialists. In language, by contrast, nearly everyone actively performs and composes.

Given their shared neurological basis, it appears
(20) that music and language evolved together as brain size increased over the course of hominid evolution. But the primacy of language over music that we can observe today suggests that language, not music, was the primary function natural selection operated on.
(25) Music, it would seem, had little adaptive value of its own, and most likely developed on the coattails of language.

Passage B

Darwin claimed that since "neither the enjoyment nor the capacity of producing musical notes are
(30) faculties of the least [practical] use to man . . . they must be ranked amongst the most mysterious with which he is endowed." I suggest that the enjoyment of and the capacity to produce musical notes are faculties of indispensable use to mothers and their infants and
(35) that it is in the emotional bonds created by the interaction of mother and child that we can discover the evolutionary origins of human music.

Even excluding lullabies, which parents sing to infants, human mothers and infants under six months
(40) of age engage in ritualized, sequential behaviors, involving vocal, facial, and bodily interactions. Using face-to-face mother-infant interactions filmed at 24 frames per second, researchers have shown that mothers and infants jointly construct mutually
(45) improvised interactions in which each partner tracks the actions of the other. Such episodes last from one-half second to three seconds and are composed of musical elements—variations in pitch, rhythm, timbre, volume, and tempo.
(50) What evolutionary advantage would such behavior have? In the course of hominid evolution, brain size increased rapidly. Contemporaneously, the increase in bipedality caused the birth canal to narrow. This resulted in hominid infants being born ever-more
(55) prematurely, leaving them much more helpless at birth. This helplessness necessitated longer, better maternal care. Under such conditions, the emotional bonds created in the premusical mother-infant interactions we observe in *Homo sapiens* today—behavior whose
(60) neurological basis essentially constitutes the capacity to make and enjoy music—would have conferred considerable evolutionary advantage.

ACKNOWLEDGEMENTS

Leslie Judd Ahlander, "Mexico's Muralists and the New York School." ©1979 by The General Secretariat of the Organization of American States.

Fred Bertram, "The Particular Problems of the Roma." ©1996 by The Regents of the University of California.

Tom Cornford, "The Freedom of Information Act 2000: Genuine or Sham?" ©2001 by Tom Cornford.

Ellen Dissanayake, "Antecedents of the Temporal Arts in Early Mother-Infant Interaction." ©2000 by the Massachusetts Institute of Technology.

James R. Elkins, "What Kind of Story Is Legal Writing?" ©1996 by Legal Studies Forum.

Dean Falk, "Hominid Brain Evolution and the Origins of Music." ©2000 by the Massachusetts Institute of Technology.

Ross Gelbspan, *The Heat is On: The Climate Crisis, The Cover-Up, The Prescription.* ©1998 by Perseus Books.

Louis P. Masur, "What It Will Take to Turn Historians Into Writers." ©2001 by The Chronicle of Higher Education.

"Offshore Production, Storage and Transportation." ©1998 by the Canada-Nova Scotia Offshore Petroleum Board.

Michael L. Parsons, *Global Warming: The Truth behind the Myth.* ©1995 by Insight Books Plenum Press.

John Sandlos, "Purple Loosestrife and the 'Bounding' of Nature in North American Wetlands." ©1997 by Electronic Journal of Sociology.

Daniel Q. Thompson, Ronald L. Stuckey, and Edith B. Thompson, "Spread, Impact, and Control of Purple Loosestrife (*Lythrum salicaria*) in North American Wetlands." ©1987 by U.S. Fish and Wildlife Service.

Mary Ellen Tsekos, "Minority Rights: The Failure of International Law to Protect the Roma." ©2002 by Human Rights Watch.

United Kingdom Parliament, "Your Right to Know: The Government's Proposals for a Freedom of Information Act." Cm 3818. 1997.

Jonathan Wills, "Muddied Waters: A Survey of Offshore Oilfield Drilling Wastes and Disposal Techniques to Reduce the Ecological Impact of Sea Dumping." ©2000 by the Sakhalin Environment Watch.

LSAT® PREP TOOLS

Save on LSAT prep with our . . .
Whole Test Prep Packages™

Each package includes SuperPrep and one of the 10 Actuals books.

Choose from four packages:

Packages I–IV: $38 online

- The Whole Test Prep Package I—SuperPrep with the 10 Actual, Official LSAT PrepTests book
- The Whole Test Prep Package II—SuperPrep with the 10 More Actual, Official LSAT PrepTests book
- The Whole Test Prep Package III—SuperPrep with The Next 10 Actual, Official LSAT PrepTests book
- The Whole Test Prep Package IV—SuperPrep with the 10 New Actual, Official LSAT PrepTests with Comparative Reading

SuperPrep is our most comprehensive LSAT preparation book. It includes:

- 3 complete PrepTests
- a guide to LSAT logic (Note: similar content in The Official LSAT Handbook)
- explanations for every item in all 3 tests (February 2000, February 1999, February 1996)
- sample Comparative Reading questions and explanations

For pure practice at a great price, you can't beat the 10 Actuals series.
Each book includes:

- 10 previously administered LSATs
- an answer key for each test
- a writing sample for each test
- score-conversion tables
- sample Comparative Reading questions and explanations

Visit our website: LSAC.org or call: 215.968.1001

LSAC.org

LSAT® Preparation

The Official LSAT SuperPrep®

SuperPrep is our most comprehensive LSAT preparation book. It includes:

- 3 complete PrepTests
- a guide to LSAT logic (Note: similar content in The Official LSAT Handbook)
- explanations for every item in all 3 tests (Feb. 2000, Feb. 1999, Feb. 1996)
- sample Comparative Reading questions and explanations

$24 online

LSAT ItemWise®

LSAC's popular, online LSAT familiarization tool, LSAT ItemWise:

- includes all three types of LSAT questions—Analytical Reasoning, Logical Reasoning, and Reading Comprehension;
- keeps track of your answers; and
- shows you explanations as to why answers are correct or incorrect.

Although it is best to use our paper-and-pencil Official LSAT PrepTest products to fully prepare for the LSAT, you can enhance your preparation by understanding all three question types and why your answers are right or wrong. ItemWise includes sample Comparative Reading questions and explanations.

$18 (unlimited access with active LSAC account)

10 Actual, Official LSAT PrepTests™

(contains PrepTests 7, 9, 10, 11, 12, 13, 14, 15, 16, 18)

10 More Actual, Official LSAT PrepTests™

(contains PrepTests 19 through 28)

The Next 10 Actual, Official LSAT PrepTests™

(contains PrepTests 29 through 38)

For pure practice at an unbelievable price, you can't beat the 10 Actuals series. Each book includes:

- 10 previously administered LSATs with answer keys, writing samples, and score-conversion tables
- sample Comparative Reading questions and explanations

$24 each online

10 New Actual, Official LSAT PrepTests with Comparative Reading™

(contains PrepTests 52 through 61)

$24 online

. . . THE SERIOUS **LAW SCHOOL APPLICANT**

The Official LSAT PrepTests®

Each PrepTest contains an actual LSAT administered on the date indicated. You can practice as if taking an actual test by following the test-taking instructions and timing yourself. In addition to actual LSAT questions, each PrepTest contains an answer key, writing sample, and score-conversion table. PrepTests 52–71 include Comparative Reading questions. Some PrepTests are available as ebooks at major etailer sites.

$8 each

The Official LSAT PrepTest 74
December 2014 LSAT
(available late January 2015)

The Official LSAT PrepTest 73
October 2014 LSAT
(available late November 2014)

The Official LSAT PrepTest 72
June 2014 LSAT
(available late July 2014)

The Official LSAT PrepTest 71
December 2013 LSAT
(available late January 2014)

The Official LSAT PrepTest 70
October 2013 LSAT
(available late November 2013)

The Official LSAT PrepTest 69
June 2013 LSAT

The Official LSAT PrepTest 68
December 2012 LSAT

The Official LSAT PrepTest 67
October 2012 LSAT

The Official LSAT PrepTest 66
June 2012 LSAT

The Official LSAT PrepTest 65
December 2011 LSAT

The Official LSAT PrepTest 64
October 2011 LSAT

The Official LSAT PrepTest 63
June 2011 LSAT

The Official LSAT PrepTest 62
December 2010 LSAT

The Official LSAT PrepTest 61
October 2010 LSAT

The Official LSAT PrepTest 60
June 2010 LSAT

The Official LSAT PrepTest 59
December 2009 LSAT

The Official LSAT PrepTest 58
September 2009 LSAT

The Official LSAT PrepTest 57
June 2009 LSAT

The Official LSAT PrepTest 56
December 2008 LSAT

The Official LSAT PrepTest 55
October 2008 LSAT

The Official LSAT PrepTest 54
June 2008 LSAT

The Official LSAT PrepTest 53
December 2007 LSAT

The Official LSAT PrepTest 52
September 2007 LSAT

NOTES:

NOTES:

NOTES:

NOTES:

NOTES:

NOTES:

NOTES: